RELATED TITLES IN THE SERIES

Nō as Performance: An Analysis of the Kuse Scene of Yamamba
Monica Bethe and Karen Brazell

Dance in the Nō Theater
Monica Bethe and Karen Brazell
Volume I, *Dance Analysis*   Volume II, *Plays and Scores*
Volume III, *Dance Patterns*
NUMBER 29 (videotapes available)

Twelve Plays of the Noh and Kyōgen Theaters
Karen Brazell, EDITOR
NUMBER 50

BUNGO MANUAL

BUNGO MANUAL

Selected Reference Materials

for Students of Classical Japanese

Helen Craig McCullough

East Asia Program
Cornell University
Ithaca, New York 14853

The *Cornell East Asia Series* publishes manuscripts on a wide variety of scholarly topics pertaining to East Asia. Manuscripts are published on the basis of camera-ready copy provided by the volume author or editor.

Inquiries should be addressed to Editorial Board, East Asia Series, East Asia Program, Cornell University, 140 Uris Hall, Ithaca, New York 14853.

PREFACE

This handbook makes no claim to originality, comprehensiveness, or professional expertise in linguistics. It merely aims to bring together useful materials from Japanese reference works in a form convenient for Western students using the classical language. The definitions and explanations derive mainly from Konishi Jin'ichi, *Kobun kenkyū hō* (Tokyo, 1973), Yuzawa Kōkichirō, *Bungo bunpō shōsetsu* (Tokyo, 1959), and Shinmura Izuru, ed., *Kōjien* (Tokyo, 1976). The illustrative quotations are drawn mainly from Konishi, *Kōjien,* and my own reading.

HCM

CONTENTS

MEANINGS AND USES OF COMMON VERBAL AND ADJECTIVAL SUFFIXES

This section discusses verbal and adjectival suffixes frequently encountered in literary Japanese (*bungo*[*tai*] 文語体, *kobun* 古文). The suffixes are attached to forms of the host words called bases, for which see Tables I–III.[1]

Most of the suffixes treated belong to the grammatical category known as *jodōshi* 助動詞. According to standard Japanese definitions, a *jodōshi* is an inflected form, incapable of independent existence, that modifies the meaning of the word to which it is suffixed. Inflected words like *gotoshi*, which would seem to most people to possess the capacity to stand alone, are regarded as belonging to the *jodōshi* category, and are so treated here. We shall further extend the term suffix to cover a number of particles (*joshi* 助詞)—*baya, ba, namu, de, ji*, and *do/domo*—which occur immediately after bases that do not ordinarily stand alone (i.e. the *mizenkei* and *izenkei*).

Auxiliary verbs—e.g. respect verbs (*tamau, tatematsuru*, etc.) and such others as *somu* (begin to) and *wataru* (keep on)—constitute one type of inflected suffix. Since they present few problems, they are not discussed in this section, but the student is advised to familiarize himself with the important respect verbs by consulting the List of Common Honorific, Polite, and Humble Verbs. All auxiliary verbs follow the *ren'yōkei*.

---

[1]To facilitate use of Japanese reference works, this handbook follows standard Japanese terminology and analytical methods in its treatment of bases.

SUFFIXES ATTACHED TO THE MIZENKEI

1. Affirmative suffixes indicating conjecture, probability, possibility, anticipation, intention, desire, suitability

    a. *Mu* and its variant form *n* (incomplete *yodan*: [ma]/—/mu, n/ mu, n/ me/ —/)

        Mu is the commonest of numerous suffixes of conjecture (*suiryō no jodōshi* 推量の助動詞), both affirmative and negative: *beshi, ji, kemu, maji, mashi, meri, mu, nari, ramu, rashi*. Some suffixes of conjecture are added to the *mizenkei* (*ji, mashi, mu*); others to the *shūshikei* (*beshi, maji, meri, nari, ramu, rashi*). One, *kemu*, follows the *ren'yōkei*, since it is actually a combination of *ki* (in its *mizenkei* form) and *mu*. Unlike some of the others (*kemu, ramu*), *mu* has no relationship to tense. Its primary meanings are as follows.

    (1) When used of the speaker's own act, it usually indicates intention or desire. MJ: *u* (*ō* or *yō*). English: "I intend to," "I am going ot," "I want to," "I will." (See also *muzu* below.)

        Examples:

            Iza koto towa*mu* miyakodori: *I'm going to* ask you something, capital-bird. (*Ise*)

            Kono miya yori tamawara*n*: *We want to* receive it from this house. (*Take.*)

            Kore hito ni hanata*n* to nan omou: I feel, indeed, that *I want to* get rid of this [child] to someone. (*Ōkagami*)

    (2) When used of an act of a third person or thing, or of an event, it is generally equivalent to MJ *darō*. It may indicate conjecture or prediction about the future, or conjecture about a present situation of which the speaker has no direct knowledge. MJ: *darō* or *ka mo shirenai*. English: "It/they probably will," "it/they perhaps."

        Examples:

harugasumi	*Might they be* ready
tanabiku yama no	To scatter from the branches—
sakurabana	Those cherry blossoms
utsurowa*mu* to ya	Now growing ever paler
iro kawariyuku	In the hills where spring haze trails? (KKS 69)

momijiba wa	I would like to fill
sode ni kokiirete	My sleeves to overflowing
moteidenamu	With red and gold leaves,
aki wa kagiri to	And carry them back to those
mi*mu* hito no tame	Who *may* think autumn is done.

(KKS 309)

(3) *Mu* may also indicate:

(a) Something natural or suitable. MJ: *ga yoi, hazu da, beki da.*
English: "would be well to," "ought to," "presumably will."

Example:

Iitojimetsuru koto wa sate koso ara*me*: Once a person has made a statement, he *ought to* stick to it. (*Mak.*)

(b) A desire on the part of the speaker to avoid a direct statement. This use is restricted to the *rentaikei* (including the *rentaikei* substantive).

Examples:

sakurairo ni	I shall dye my robe
koromo wa fukaku	Carefully in the color
somete kimu	Of cherry blossoms
hana no chirina*mu*	And wear it as a keepsake
nochi no katami ni	After the flowers [*perhaps*] scatter. (KKS 66)

Koishikara*mu* oriori, toriidete mitamae: Please take it out and look at it whenever you *may* feel lonely. (*Take.*)

(c) With an interrogative particle, a rhetorical question.

Example:

Sono toki kuyu tomo, kai ara*n* ya: Even if he does feel regret then, what good will it do? (TZG)

(d) A general statement, or a speculation about a hypothetical situation. This use is also restricted to the *rentaikei*.

Examples:

Saiin yori onfumi no saburawa*n* ni wa, ika de ka isogiageha-berazaran: If there is a letter from the Kamo Virgin, is anyone likely to fail to present it with all possible speed? (*Mak.*)

Kari sunadori nando no yō ni, ashidachi no yokarō kata e wa mukawa*n*, ashikarō kata e wa mukawaji nando sōrawa*n* ni wa, ikusa ni katsu koto yomo sōrawaji: As in hunting, fishing, and the like, so in war, we can never win if we head toward places that seem convenient and avoid those that seem inconvenient. (*Heike*)

3

(e) When used of an act of the person(s) addressed, *mu* may convey a suggestion, request, exhortation, or polite imperative. MJ: *shitara dō desu ka*; *shimasen ka*; *shite kudasai*. English: "How about doing?" "Won't you?" "Please."

Example:

> Sesshōdono yori, "Zonji no mune araba ikutabi mo sōmon ni koso oyoba*me*" to ōsekudasarekeredomo, issetsu mochiitatematsurazu: The Regent told them, "If you have anything on your minds, *you should* report it to the throne as often as you please," but they paid no attention. (*Heike*)

b. *Mashi* (irreg.: mase, mashika/—/mashi/mashi/mashika [does not occur with *ba*]/—/)

Meanings:

(1) Conjecture about a situation contrary to fact. MJ: *moshi . . . de attara*. English: "If such-and-such a situation were to exist, or had existed, then probably."

Mashi will normally appear in the second clause of the conjecture, where it can usually be translated "would." The *mizenkei* (*mase* before the Heian period; *mashika* from the ninth century on) may appear with *ba* in the first clause, where its meaning is "if," "supposing that." In such cases, the second-clause *mashi* is occasionally replaced by another suffix, such as *mu* or *beshi*. Other typical constructions: *-seba . . .-mashi*; *naku wa . . . -mashi*; *naraba . . .-mashi*.

Sometimes only one element of the hypothesis is explicitly stated. Thus in the last example below, the "if" clause is merely implied—"if it were possible." In such a context, *mashi* may contain an added element of desire or command.

Examples:

omoitsutsu	Did he come to me
nureba ya hito no	Because I dropped off to sleep
mietsuramu	Tormented by longing?
yume to shiriseba	Had I but known that I dreamed,
samezara*mashi* o	I *would not have* awakened.

(KKS 552)

Kakarubeshi to dani shiritariseba, Imai o Seta e wa yarazara-*mashi*: *If* only I had known it would be like this, I *would not have* sent Imai to Seta. (*Heike*)

inochi dani	If life were to last
kokoro ni kanau	For as long as we saw fit,
mono naraba	Would we be likely
nani ka wakare no	To suffer such deep distress
kanashikara*mashi*	Just because of a parting? (KKS 387)

4

Kari ni ima kono fumi o hirogeza*ramashikaba*, kono koto o shira*n* ya: If we had not opened this text now, *would* we have been aware of this fact? (TZG)

miru hito mo	Blossoming cherries
naki yamazato no	At the mountain villages
sakurabana	With none to see them:
hoka no chiri*namu*	*Would that* they might not flower
nochi zo saka*mashi*	Until others had scattered! (KKS 68)

(2) Intention, desire, simple presumption, conjecture, suitability, or rhetorical question—i.e. meanings paralleling those of *mu*. Ordinarily follows an interrogative or dubitative form.

Examples:

Shikibukyō no miya, hōshi ni ya narina*mashi* to oboesedo: The Prince-Minister of Ceremonial thought that he might *like to* become a monk, but. . . (*Eiga monogatari*)

Kore o ika ni shite ite kudara*mashi*: How can I manage to take this [child] with me when I go? (*Ochikubo monogatari*)

c. *Muzu, nzu, uzu* (incomplete *sahen*: /—/ /—/ muzu, nzu, uzu/ muzuru, nzuru, uzuru/ muzure, nzure, uzure/ —/)

Muzu and its variants *nzu* and *uzu* are contractions of -*mu to su*. Their meanings are similar to, but more emphatic than, those of *mu*. MJ: *shiyō to suru*; *deshō*; *to omowareru*. English: "I will," "probably," "certainly," "I intend to."

Examples:

Izuchi mo izuchi mo ashi no mukitaramu kata e ina*muzu*: We *might as well* head (i.e. we intend to head) in whatever direction our feet happen to point. (*Take.*)

Mukae ni hitobito mōdeko*muzu*: People will *surely* come to fetch me. (*Take.*)

d. *Baya* (particle)

The particle *baya*, which follows the *mizenkei*, can be regarded as a desiderative suffix. (Do not confuse with -*ba ya* after the *izenkei*, a construction in which *ya* functions as an interrogative particle.) *Baya* has the following meanings.

(1) Desire on the part of the speaker for the unlikely or impossible. MJ: *dekitara nā; nara mā*. English: "If only," "Would that."

Examples:

satsuki koba	If the Fifth Month comes,
naki mo furinan	We may have more than enough,
hototogisu	Cuckoo, of your song.
masashiki hodo no	I would like to hear your voice
koe o kika*baya*	Before your season begins.
	(KKS 138)

Yokarō taishōgun ni kuma*baya*: *If only I might* grapple with
a worthy general! (*Heike*)

(2) Temperate expression of the speaker's will. MJ: *shiyō; -tai mono
da*. English: "I intend to," "I want to." Occurs in post-Heian
texts.

Example:
Takasago no ura o mo ikken se*baya* to zonjisōrau: *I intend to*
have a look at Takasago shore, too. (Nō, "Takasago")

e. *Mahoshi* (shiku-type adj.: mahoshiku/mahoshiku/mahoshi/mahoshiki/
mahoshikere/—/)
Mahoshi, a desiderative suffix, has the following uses.
(1) It ordinarily indicates desire on the part of the speaker.
MJ: *-tai; -te hoshii*. English: "I wish," "I prefer," "I would
like."

Examples:
Okina no toshi koso kika*mahoshikere: I would like to* ask your
age, old man. (*Ōkagami*)
Hichiriki wa ito kashigamashiku. . . kejikaku kika*mahoshi-
karazu*: The oboe is very noisy. . . I have *no desire to* (or:
I prefer not to) hear it close by. (*Mak.*)

(2) It occurs infrequently to indicate desire on the part of someone
other than the speaker. MJ: *-tagaru*.

Example:
Ge ni ira*mahoshiki* koto ni haberedo: It was natural that they
should have wished to participate, but. . . (*Ōkagami*)

Note: The expression *aramahoshi* means "ideal," "perfect." Nani mo motade
zo *aramahoshiki*: The *ideal situation* is to have no belongings. (TZG)

f. *Ba* (particle)
When *ba* follows the *mizenkei*, it can be regarded as an uninflected
suffix of hypothesis. It indicates that the preceding sequence is a pro-
visional condition of the following sequence. MJ: *nara; tara*. English:
"If."

Examples:

natsuyama ni	O cuckoo singing
naku hototogisu	Amid the summer mountains:
kokoro ara*ba*	*If* you have feelings,
monoomou ware ni	Do not harrow with your voice
koe na kikase so	One whose heart already aches.

(KKS 145)

6

Uemon no kami shizuma*ba*, ware mo shizumamu: *If* Uemon no Kami drowns, I, too, will drown. (*Heike*)

Tsuyu mo, mono sora ni kakera*ba*, futo ikoroshitamae: If anything at all flies high in the sky, shoot it to death at once. (*Take*.)

Uchi ni mairasena*ba*, e mōsasetamawaji: *If* he goes to the palace, you probably won't be able to speak to him. (*Ōkagami*)

g. *Namu* (particle)

When *namu* follows the *mizenkei*, it indicates a hope or demand directed by the speaker toward a person or thing other than himself. (Do not confuse with the emphatic particle *namu*, or with the combination formed by the *mizenkei* of *nu* plus *mu*.)

Example:

kotoshi yori	Blossoming cherry
haru shirisomuru	Who have just this year begun
sakurabana	To know what spring is:
chiru to iu koto wa	*Would that you might* never learn
narawazara*namu*	The meaning of scattering. (KKS 49)

2. Negative suffixes (*uchikeshi no jodōshi* 打消しの助動詞, *hitei no jodōshi* 否定 の助動詞)

a. *Zu* (irregular: [na], zu/ zu/ zu/ nu/ ne/ —/)

Zu and its derivative *zari* are by far the commonest negative suffixes in literary Japanese. Both are unqualified negatives. MJ: *nai; nu (n)*.

Examples:

Kata tōki wa, e tsugeyara*zu*: We could *not* send word to those who were distant. (*Mak.*)

Miya no nyōbō ni otora*nu* sama no sōzoku: Costumes *not* inferior in appearance to those of the Empress's ladies-in-waiting.

(*Eiga monogatari*)

Taishō ni ara*nedomo*: Although he was *not* a Major Captain. . .

(*Heike*)

Kamishimo o eraba*zu* waka o shō sesasetamawan ni: Since His Majesty intended to appraise the poems *without* regard to status . . . (*Ōkagami*)

b. *Zari* (incomplete *rahen*: zara/ zari/ —/ zaru/ zare/ zare/)

Zari, a contraction of *zu ari*, (1) usually occurs instead of *zu* in the *mizenkei* form, (2) always replaces *zu* in the *meireikei*, and (3) *may* occur instead of *zu* in any other form except the *shūshikei*. MJ: *naide iru*.

Examples:

Narabubeku mo ara*zari*kereba: Since it was *not* likely that he could compare. . . (*Genji*)

7

omoitsutsu	Did he come to me
nureba ya hito no	Because I dropped off to sleep
mietsuran	Tormented by love?
yume to shiriseba	Had I but known that I dreamed,
same*zara*mashi o	I would *not* have awakened.

(KKS 552)

c. *De* (uninflected)

Although technically classified as a conjunctive particle (*setsuzoku joshi* 接続助詞), *de* can be regarded as a suffix. It is a contraction of *zute*—i.e. of the *ren'yōkei* of the simple negative *zu* plus the conjunctive particle *te*. MJ: *naide*. English: "without."

Examples:

mate to iu ni	If, when we said, "Wait,"
chira*de* shi tomaru	They held fast to their branches,
mono naraba	*Never* scattering,
nani o sakura ni	What could anyone prefer
omoimasamashi	To blossoms of the cherry? (KKS 70)

Fukaki kokorozashi o shira*de* wa aigatashi to namu omou: I feel that it is impossible for me to marry *without* knowing how sincere [the man's] feelings are. (*Take.*)

d. *Ji* (uninflected)

Ji, classified as a particle, is known to occur only in *shūshikei*, *rentaikei*, and, rarely, *izenkei* position. Its meanings are the negative opposite numbers of the main meanings of *mu*.

(1) It may indicate the subject's negative intention, resolve, or desire. In that case, the subject is always either the speaker ("I") or something closely related to him (e.g. "my tears"). MJ: verb plus *nai tsumori da; -mai*. English: "I do not intend to," "I do not wish to," etc.

Examples:

Yomo katarari tora*ji*: *I have no intention* at all of weaning her away from you. (*Mak.*)

Hakabakashiku wa arase*ji*: *I will never* let them lead a happy life. (*Ōkagami*)

(2) It may indicate negative conjecture about an event, or about an act of another person. MJ: *nai darō; -mai*. English: "probably not," "perhaps not," "I think not."

Examples:

Isshō no haji kore ni suguru wa ara*ji*: *No other* humiliation in the course of my lifetime *could possibly* exceed this. (*Take.*)

Hōshi bakari urayamashikaranu mono wa ara*ji*: There is *probably nobody* less to be envied than a monk. (TZG)

e. *Maji*

For this suffix, sometimes added to the *mizenkei* of *kamiichidan* and *kaminidan* verbs, see the section on *shūshikei* suffixes.

3. The *ru/raru* suffix (*shimo nidan*; see Table IV for verb categories to which attached)

Ru and *raru* may be considered alternative forms of a single suffix, which has the meanings and uses listed below.

Note: In texts of the Nara period, the *ru/raru* suffix appears less frequently than *yu/rayu*, a *shimo nidan* suffix with uses identical to the first three below. *Yu/rayu* is seldom encountered in later texts.

a. Passive use (*ukemi* 受身). MJ: *reru/rareru*

Example:
Nusubito narikereba, kuni no kami ni karame*rare*nikeri: Since he *was a thief, he *was arrested* by the provincial governor. (*Ise*)

b. Potential use (*kanō* 可能). MJ: *suru koto ga dekiru*. English: "can," "be able to."

Example:
Nukan to suru ni, ōkata nuka*rezu*: When he tried to get it off, he *could* not get it off at all. (TZG).

c. Spontaneity use: action occurring without conscious volition (*shizen kanō* 自然可能, *jihatsu* 自発). MJ: *shizen ni. . . .-rareru*; *shizen ni. . . shite shimau.* English: "naturally," "spontaneously." Sometimes untranslatable.

Examples:
Tsukuyo ni wa konu hito mata*ru*: On a moonlit night, *I find myself awaiting one who will not come.* (KKS 775)

Toki no ma no keburi to mo narinan to zo uchimiru yori omowa*ruru:* The moment one glances at it, one *instinctively* thinks, "It will undoubtedly become transient smoke." (TZG)

Kyō wa miyako nomi zo omoiyara*ruru:* The capital *keeps coming into my mind* today. (*Tosa*)

d. Honorific use (*sonkei* 尊敬). Shows respect of writer or speaker for subject of verb. MJ: *-reru/rareru*; *o-. . . ni naru.*

Examples:
Ue . . . kuchioshū oboshimesa*ru*: His Majesty considered it regrettable. (*Eiga monogatari*)

Minken no mazushiki koto o oboshite, mitose no mitsugi o todome*ra*renu: Taking cognizance of the people's poverty, the Emperor stopped the taxes for three years. (*Jinnō shōtōki*)

Katara*re*yo: Tell about it. (*Ōkagami*)

9

4. Causative suffixes
   a. The *su/sasu* suffix (*shimo nidan*; see Table IV for verb categories to which attached)

   Like *ru* and *raru*, *su* and *sasu* may be considered alternative forms of the same suffix, which has the uses listed below.

   (1) Causative use (*shieki* 使役). MJ: *seru/saseru*. English: "cause to," "have," "allow."

   Note that there are two English meanings, "cause" and "allow," for the Japanese causative. It will sometimes be necessary to choose between them on the basis of context.

   Examples:
   Dairi o yaka*se*tsuru koto koso yasukarane:
   It was terrible that we *let* them burn the palace. (*Heike*)
   Mizuguruma o tsukura*se*rarekeri: His Majesty *had* them make a waterwheel. (TZG)
   Tsuki no miyako no hito mōdekoba, torae*sase*temu:
   If people from the Moon Palace come, I'll *have* [my men] capture them. (*Take*)

   (2) Honorific use (*sonkei* 尊敬). MJ: *o-. . . ni naru*. When used in this sense, *su/sasu* usually either (1) follows a verb that is itself honorific (such as *notamau*, an honorific equivalent of *iu*, say), or (2) precedes the honorific auxiliary verb *tamau*. In the latter case, the resultant forms, *-setamau* and *-sasetamau*, are highly honorific, and in ordinary written prose are usually reserved for members of the imperial or shogunal court. (The usage in quoted conversation is somewhat broader.) *Su/sasu* is more honorific than *ru/raru*. See also *Shimu* below.

   Examples:
   Goranjite imijū odoroka*se*tamau: His Majesty saw and was exceedingly surprised. (*Mak.*)
   Ito imijū mede*sase*tamaite mono kazuke*sase*tamaiki:
   His Majesty praised her extravagantly and gave her a present. (*Ōkagami*)
   Kaera*se*tamae to iu: "Return," he said. (*Heike*)

b. Shimu (*shimo nidan*: shime/ shime/ shimu/ shimuru/ shimure/ shime/)
   Shimu, which has the same main uses as *su/sasu*, occurs frequently in texts of the Nara and medieval (*chūsei*) periods. Although it is almost never encountered in the works of Heian women, it appears in Chinese-language (*kanbun*), Chinese-influenced, and other works by Heian male authors. In texts of the late Heian period, it sometimes appears after the *mizenkei* of a humble verb, in which case its role is said to be that of an intensifier.

10

(1) Causative use (*shieki* 使役)

Examples:

Mi o yaburu yori mo, kokoro o itama*shimuru* wa, hito o sokonau koto nao hanahadashi: It does much more harm to *wound* someone's heart than to injure his body. (TZG)

Tsurayuki meshiidete, uta tsukōmatsura*shime*tamaeri: His Majesty called Tsurayuki over and *had* him compose a poem. (*Ōkagami*)

(2) Honorific use (*sonkei* 尊敬) (Heian on)

When used as an honorific, *shimu* tends to appear as a compound with *tamau*. The combination ranks with *se/sasetamau* as the acme of exaltation.

Example:

Akashi no umaya to iu tokoro ni on-yadori se*shime*tamaite: He lodged at a place called Akashi post station . . . (*Ōkagami*)

5. [F]u

This suffix, which occurs mostly with *yodan* verbs, makes a new *shimo nidan* verb indicating repetition or continuation. It was common in the Nara period, but later tended to be restricted to specific verbs, such as *chiru* and *nageku*. It gradually disappeared.

Example:

Ōna nurigome no uchi ni Kaguyahime o idaka*ete* ori: The old woman *was* hold*ing* Kaguyahime in her arms inside the storeroom. (*Take.*)

SUFFIXES ATTACHED TO THE REN'YŌKEI

1. Suffixes of completion or positive affirmation (*kanryō no jodōshi* 完了の助動詞, *kakujutsu no jodōshi* 確述の助動詞)

   Nu, tsu, and *tari,* the *ren'yōkei* suffixes in this category, all indicate (1) definite completion of an actual or hypothetical act or state or (2) definite affirmation of, or emphatic stress on, an act or state.

   a. *Nu* (*nahen*: na/ ni/ nu/ nuru/ nure/ ne/)

   Nu is most often, but by no means invariably, found affixed to intransitive or stative verbs. Thus: nari*nu* (from *naru,* become), saki*nu* (from *saku,* bloom). It may mean:

   (1) Definite completion of an actual or hypothetical past or future act or state. Future hypothetical occurrences are relatively infrequent.

      Examples:
      Mina nori*nu*: We all got in. (*Mak.*)
      Ame makoto ni furi*nu*: The rain fell in earnest. (*Mak.*)
      Sono hi ni nari*nure*ba: When that day came . . .
                                      (*Eiga monogatari*)

   (2) Affirmation of, and emphasis on, an act or state. Often followed by *beshi, mu, ramu,* or *rashi.* MJ: *kitto. . . suru de arō; tashika ni. . . suru; shite shimau.* English: "certainly," "definitely." (The force of *nu* can sometimes be shown in English by an intensifying adverb: "finish off," "eat up.")

      Examples:
      Ikasama ni mo kondo no ikusa ni wa sōi naku kachi*nu* to oboyuru zo: I feel sure I will [*definitely*] win the battle I am about to fight. (*Heike*)
      Iza sakura, ware mo chiri*namu*: I, too, would like to scatter *completely away*, cherry blossoms. (KKS 77)

   Note that *nu* is not primarily a tense suffix. Rather, it tends to acquire a tense significance because of the fact that when an act is positively performed it may also be completely performed.

   b. *Tsu* (*shimo nidan*: te/ te/ tsu/ tsuru/ tsure/ te/)

   Tsu is generally equivalent in meaning to *nu* (which see), but it occurs primarily with verbs describing actions, rather than states, and there-

12

fore is usually found with transitive or action verbs. Thus: kaki*tsu* (from *kaku*, write), kiki*tsu* (from *kiku*, hear). It may mean:

(1) Definite completion of an act or state

> Examples:
>> Koyoi yume ni nan mietamai*tsuru*: You [*definitely*] appeared to me in a dream tonight. (*Ise*)
>> Okuretaru hitobito matsu tote, soko ni hi o kurashi*tsu*: Thinking we would wait for those who had fallen behind, we spent the [*whole*] day there. (*Sarashina nikki*)

(2) Affirmation of, and emphasis on, an act or state

> Examples:
>> Kono sake o nomi*temu* tote: Thinking that they wanted to drink *up* this wine. . . (*Ise*)
>> Hae koso nikuki mono no uchi ni ire*tsu*bekere: We must *definitely* include flies among hateful things. (*Mak.*)

c. *Tari* (*rahen*: ra/ ri/ ri/ ru/ re/ re/)

Tari has three uses, which tend to overlap. It may indicate:

(1) Completion of an act or process

> Examples:
>> Hitachi no suke to tsuke*tari*: We named her Hitachi no Suke. (*Mak.*)
>> Kuramochi no miko owashi*tari* to tsugu: Someone announced that Prince Kuramochi *had come*. (*Take.*)

(2) Continuation of the result of a completed act or state. The verb is usually, but not always, transitive. MJ: transitive verb plus *-te aru* (e.g. *akete aru*); intransitive verb plus *-te iru* (e.g. *aite iru*); *-ta*; *-ta koto ga aru*. English: past tense, perfect tense (e.g. "has opened"), or past perfect (pluperfect) tense ("had opened").

> Examples:
>> Mamoritatakaubeki shitakumi o shi*tari* tomo: Even though you *have made* preparations for a defensive fight. . . (*Take.*)
>> Uta o hito no moto ni yari*taru* ni, kaeshi senu: One *has sent* a poem to somebody, but he makes no reply. (*Mak.*)

(3) Continuation of an act or state. MJ: *-te iru*; *-te aru*. English: progressive tense ("is shining") or imperfect tense ("was shining").

> Examples:
>> Tsutsu no naka hikari*tari*: The inside of the stalk *was shining*. (*Take.*)
>> Shiniire*tari*kereba: Since he *was* in a deathly coma. . . (*Ise*)

13

> Note: This *tari* is a contraction of *-te ari*. It should not be confnsed with the "designation" (*shitei* 指定) suffix *tari* (MJ: *de aru*), a contraction of *to ari*, which follows substantives. The *shitei tari* is rarely encountered in pure Heian Japanese, but becomes common from the thirteenth century on.

2. *Ki* (irregular: ke, se/ —/ ki/ shi/ shika/ —/). See also Table IV for irregular forms with *ku* and *su*.

Principal meanings:

a. *Ki* is often classified as a past-tense suffix(*kako no jodōshi* 過去の助動詞), a definition that seems adequate for its use in some contexts.

> Examples:
> Imo ga mi*shi* ōchi no hana wa chirinubeshi: The China-tree flowers my sweetheart *saw* will surely scatter. (MYS)
> Gan Kai mo fukō ari*ki*: [Confucius's disciple] Yen Hui, too, suffer*ed* ill fortune. (TZG)

b. Particularly in the Nara and Heian periods, the tense element is usually linked to the speaker's recollection of a personal experience, a fact recognized in the alternative label "suffix of recollection" (*kaisō no jodōshi* 回想の助動詞).

> Examples:
> Oni no yō naru mono idekite korosan to shi*ki*: Creatures like demons appeared and tried to kill us. (*Take.*)
> Kono eda o orite*shika*ba: When I broke off this branch. . . (Take.)
>
> | tsui ni yuku | Upon this pathway, |
> | michi to wa kanete | *I have* long *heard* others say, |
> | kiki*shika*do | Man sets forth at last— |
> | kinō kyō to wa | Yet I had not thought to go |
> | omowazarishi o | So very soon as today. (KKS 861) |

c. *Ki* may sometimes indicate continuation of an act or process, or of the result of an act or process. This relatively rare use seems to date from the late Heian period.

> Example:
> Waga sono ni saki*shi* hana o miwataseba: When I look out on the flowers that *have bloomed* in my garden. . .
>
> (*Tametadashū*, twelfth c.)

Notes:

1. When the *mizenkei* (*se*) is followed by *ba*, this suffix, like *mashi*, indicates conjecture about a hypothetical situation. See the first and second examples under *mashi* (1), p. 4.

2. When the *rentaikei* (*shi*) occurs at the end of a sentence without *kakarimusubi* (p. 71):

a. It may indicate that something emphatic, often with a hint of sadness, has been left unsaid. MJ: *koto yo*; *koto da nā*. (See also Suffixes Attached to the Rentaikei, note on *rentaidome*.)

Examples:
> Mukashimonogatari-mekite oboehaberi*shi*: I felt that it was like something in an old romance. . . (*Genji*)
> Akatoki tsuyu ni wa ga tachinure*shi*: *Ah!* I stood drenched in the morning dew. (MYS 105)

b. It may function as an ordinary *shūshikei*. (Chiefly post-Heian)

Example:
> Ikku o hashira ni nokoshihaberi*shi*: I left a stanza on a pillar. (*Oku no hosomichi*)

3. *Keri* (incomplete *rahen*: kera/ —/ keri/ keru/ kere/ —/)
Keri is conjectured to be a contraction either of *ki* 来, the *ren'yōkei* of *ku* (come), plus *ari*, or of the *jodōshi ki* plus *ari*. Like the *jodōshi ki* (see 2 above), it is usually described as a past-tense (*kako* 過去) or recollection (*kaisō* 回想) suffix, the rationale in the latter case being that it indicates recollection of something learned second-hand, rather than first-hand as with *ki*. In actual practice, it usually seems to contain a mixture of tense, durative, and/or exclamatory elements. The meanings listed below should not be considered mutually exclusive. Principal meanings:

a. Continuation of an act or state initiated in the past. MJ: *-te kita*; *-te kite iru*. English: progressive tense; perfect tense.

Example:
Kamiyo yori	The thing that has been said
Iitsute kuraku	Since the age of the gods:
Sora mitsu	*It has been handed down,*
Yamato no kuni wa	Said for generations,
Sumekami no	That the land of Yamato
Itsukushiki kuni	Is a land
Kotodama no	Where sovereign gods wield power,
Sakihau kuni to	A land with the fortune
Kataritsugi	Of mighty words. . . (MYS 894)
Iitsugai*keri*	

b. (Chiefly to late Heian) Presentation of information about the past acquired from tradition, hearsay, or some other second-hand source, or invented by the author. MJ: *-ta*; *-ta sō da*. English: past tense.

Examples:
> Ima wa mukashi, taketori no okina to iu mono ari*keri*: Once long ago there was somebody called "the old bamboo-cutter." (*Take.*)

Mukashi, otoko, Musashi no kuni made madoiariki*keri*: Once a man wandered as far as the province of Musashi. (*Ise*)

c. (Chiefly to late Heian) It may indicate a feeling of surprise or wonder evoked by the speaker's sudden awareness of a continuing condition or situation which he had not noticed before. MJ: (*ki ga tsuite miru to*) . . . *nan da nā*; . . . *dattake*. English: exclamation point (often untranslatable). This is the usual meaning when *keri* occurs in Heian poetry.

Examples:

yuku mizu ni	Less profitable
kazu kaku yori mo	Than writing on the waters
hakanaki wa	Of a flowing stream—
omowanu hito o	Such is the futility
omou nari*keri*	Of unrequited passion! (KKS 522)
utsusemi no	How like this fleeting
yo ni mo nitaru ka	Cicada-husk world of ours!
hanazakura	The moment we see
saku to mishi ma ni	The cherry trees in blossom,
katsu chirini*keri*	All their petals have scattered! (KKS 73)

d. (Haikai poetry) Simple exclamation

Example:
Kareeda ni karasu no tomari*keri*: A crow resting on a dead branch! (Bashō)

4. *Kemu, ken* (incomplete *yodan*: —/ —/ kemu, ken/ kemu, ken/ keme/ —/)

Kemu (or *ken*), thought by some scholars to be a combination of the suffixes *ki* (2 above) and *mu*, indicates conjecture or hearsay about the past. Meanings:

a. Conjecture about a past act or state, often with specific reference to cause, reason, degree, time, place, method, person(s) involved, etc. Often appears with an interrogative or dubitative particle; often takes the form of a parenthetical remark (*hasamikomi* 挟み込み). MJ: -*ta darō*. English: "must have," "probably did," etc.

Examples:

tori ga naku	How sad *must have been* the parting
azumaotoko no	From his wife
tsuma-wakare	Of the man from the cock-crowing East,
kanashiku ari*kemu*	For long indeed
toshi no o nagami	Will be the years of separation. (MYS 4333)

16

kimi ya koshi	Did you, I wonder, come here,
ware ya yuki*kemu*	Or *might I have* gone there?
omōezu	I scarcely know. . .
yume ka utsutsu ka	Was it dream or reality?
nete ka samete ka	Did I sleep or wake? (*Ise*)

Sasaki Shirō Takatsuna ga itomamōshi ni maitarikeru ni, Kamakura-dono ikaga oboshimesare*ken*. . . Ikezuki o Sasaki ni tabu: When Sasaki Shirō Takatsuna went to take his leave, the Lord of Kamakura (what *might he have* had in his mind?) gave Ikezuki [name of a horse] to Sasaki. (*Heike*)

b. Hearsay about the past; speaker is not certain of his facts. MJ: *-ta to iu*; *-ta to ka iu koto da.* (Limited to *rentaikei.*)

Example:
Furu no taki wa, hōō no goranji ni owashimashi*ken* koso medetakere: How splendid that a retired sovereign in holy orders should *apparently have gone* [as I have heard he did] to see Furu Waterfall!
(*Mak.*)

17

SUFFIXES ATTACHED TO THE SHŪSHIKEI

The six suffixes attached to the *shūshikei* in literary Japanese are all described by grammarians as suffixes of conjecture (*suiryō no jodōshi* 推量の助動詞). Five are affirmative; one, *maji*, is negative.

These suffixes regularly follow the *rentaikei*, rather than the *shūshikei*, of *rahen* verbs and *rahen* suffixes. They may also sometimes be encountered after the *mizenkei* of *kamiichidan* and *kaminidan* verbs. When attached to adjectives, they normally follow the extended *rentaikei -karu* (e.g. *yokarubeshi*, not *yoshibeshi*).

1. *Beshi* (see Table IV for bases)

Beshi indicates firm, or rationally justified, expectation based on circumstance or reason, or on what is natural, fitting, or proper. It has a variety of uses, but in all except one (e below) it can usually be translated by some form of "expect."

Meanings:

a. Conjecture. MJ: *kitto . . . darō*; *ni chigainai*. English: "undoubtedly," "must."

> Examples:
> Ware wa kono miko ni makenu*beshi*: I will *surely* be defeated by this prince. (*Take*.)
> Kakuroe nite yū naru uta o yomiidasan dani ito murai ni haberu*beki*: It would *undoubtedly* be very rude merely to stay in concealment and then produce an excellent poem. (*Ōkagami*)
>
> Note: For the use of the *rentaikei beki* here, see Suffixes Attached to the Rentaikei, note on *rentaidome*.

b. Expectation based on circumstance or reason. MJ: inflected form plus *-sō da* (e.g. *ame ga furisō da*); inflected form plus *koto ni natte iru*; inflected form plus *yotei da*. English: "looks as though it will," "supposed to," "expect."

> Examples:
> Kannazuki ni Suzakuin no gyōkō aru*beshi*: The Emperor *was to* visit Suzakuin in the Tenth Month. (*Genji*)
> Sumu tachi yori idete, fune ni noru*beki* tokoro e wataru: He left his official residence and went to the place where he *was supposed to* board the vessel. (*Tosa*)

18

c. Expectation based on what is natural, fitting, or proper. MJ: *no ga mottomo da*; *hazu da*; *nakereba naranai*. English: "be right to," "ought to," "should."

Examples:
> Sabakari no mono o chikō meshiyosete chokuroku tamawasu*beki* koto naranedomo: Although it was not *appropriate* to call a person of that status close and give him an imperial reward. . . (*Ōkagami*)
> Osoru*beku* tsutsushimu*beki* wa kono madoi nari: It is this delusion that we *must* fear, that we *must* avoid. (TZG)

Note: In this sense, *beshi* sometimes functions as an imperative. The use is said to be limited to the *shūshikei*.

Example:
> Isogimairu*beshi*: Make haste to eat it. (*Heike*)

d. Intention. MJ: *shiyō to omou*; *tsumori da*. English: "intend to," "will," "would." The use is said to be limited to the *shūshikei*.

Examples:
> Kono o-uma de Ujigawa no massaki watashisōrau*beshi*: On this horse, I *intend to* [expect to] be first across the Uji River. (*Heike*)

aki no no ni	Though not journeying,
yadori wa *subeshi*	I *will* seek shelter tonight
ominaeshi	In an autumn field,
na o mutsumajimi	Drawn by the intimacy
tabi naranaku ni	Of the maidenflower's name.
	(KKS 228)

e. Potential. MJ: *koto ga dekiru*; *koto ga dekiru darō*. English: "can," "could," "probably can," "probably could."

Example:
> Kakitsukusu*beki* ni arazu: I *cannot* write a full account.
> (*Eiga monogatari*)

2. *Rashi* (—/ —/ rashi/ rashi, rashiki/ rashi, rashikere/ —/)
In Heian texts, in classical poetry of all periods, and in prose works that imitate Heian usage, *rashi* indicates a much stronger degree of certainty than MJ *rashii* (which probably dates from around the seventeenth century). It is one of the most self-confident of the *suiryō* suffixes.
Meanings:
a. *Rashi* may indicate conjecture based on objective circumstances (as contrasted with the more subjective *meri* below). The speaker, on rational grounds, draws a conclusion about something for which he has no direct visual evidence.

Examples:

miyoshino no	The white flakes of snow
yama no shirayuki	In fair Yoshino's mountains
tsumoru*rashi*	*Must* be piling high,
furusato samuku	For cold strikes ever sharper
narimasaru nari	At the ancient capital. (KKS 325)
miyama ni wa	Deep in the mountains
arare furu*rashi*	The hailstones *must* be flying,
toyama naru	For in our own hills,
masaki no kazura	Close to men's habitations,
irozukinikeri	The vines have turned to scarlet.
	(KKS 1077)

b. When a fact or situation is directly observed by the speaker, *rashi* may indicate speculation about cause, reason, time, place, method, degree, etc.

Example:

Kita no kata no koto ni yori, yo no oboe mo otoritamau*rashi*: It *seems to be because* of his wife that he has become less popular. (*Ōkagami*)

3. *Meri* (incomplete *rahen*: —/ meri/ meri/ meru/ mere/ —/)

Meri is thought to be a contraction of either *mie ari* or *mi ari*. Either derivation would suggest confident conjecture based on first-hand visual evidence. In actual usage, however, *meri* represents a highly tentative surmise. It may be regarded as standing at the opposite end of the spectrum from *rashi*.

Note: The common form *nameri* is a contraction of *naru meri*.

Meanings:

a. *Meri* usually indicates that the speaker, though basing his statement on objective evidence, hesitates to commit himself to a positive position. It may show genuine uncertainty or simply function as a device to soften the language. MJ: *yō na guai da*. English: "probably," "possibly," "seems to."

Examples:

Uruwashiki kawa na*meri*: It *seems to* be beautiful fur. (*Take.*)

Kono yo ni umarete wa, negawashikarubeki koto koso ōka*mere*: It *seems* that people find many things to desire once they have been born into this world. (TZG)

Naishi no moto e wa, tokidoki makaru*meri*ki: I recall that [my wife] (*it seems*) occasionally visited Naishi. (*Ōkagami*)

Tadaima wa nagon ni namu haberu*meru*: At present I am a Counselor. (*Utsubo monogatari*) (A response to an inquiry about the speaker's current official position. The effect of *meri* here is comparable to that of MJ final *ga* in a similar context.)

b. *Meri* may indicate subjective conjecture about the cause or reason for a fact or situation. MJ: *dōmo . . . rashii; [jibun ni wa] . . . no yō ni uketoreru.* English: "It seems to me that perhaps."

Example:
> Narimasa. . . yobe no koto ni medete irinitarikeruna*meri*: *I think it was probably because* Narimasa was impressed by what happened last night that he came [to your room]. *(Mak.)*

4. *Ramu* and its variant *ran* (Kamakura period on: also appears as *rō*). (incomplete *yodan*: —/ —/ ramu, ran/ ramu, ran/ rame/ —/)
Ramu is basically a suffix indicating conjecture about the present. It resembles *rashi* but is more subjective—i.e. when *ramu* is used there tends to be less objective justification for the conjecture than in the case of *rashi*. It occurs most frequently in *shūshikei* form.
(Note: In post-Heian texts, *ramu* may indicate simple conjecture unrelated to time.)

Meanings:
a. Conjecture about a presently existing situation of which the speaker has no direct knowledge. MJ: *[ima goro wa] . . . -te iru darō.* English: "probably is," "may be."

Examples:
> Genji no senjin wa mukōtaru wa; sadamete ōzei nite zo aru*ran*: The Genji vanguard is moving toward us; they *must have* a large army. *(Heike)*
> Mizukara wa imiji to omou*ramedo*: Although they *probably* think of themselves as important. . . (TZG)

b. When a fact or situation is directly observed by the speaker, *ramu*, like *rashi*, may indicate speculation about cause, reason, time, place, method, degree, etc. As in the third example below, there is sometimes an unspoken "why" that must be supplied by the translator. MJ: *-te iru no darō; dōshite darō.* English: "probably," "I wonder why."

Examples:

hisakata no	*Might it be because*
tsuki no katsura mo	The cassia tree in the moon
aki wa nao	Yellows in autumn
momiji sureba ya	That the celestial orb
terimasaru*ramu*	Shines with this new brilliance?
	(KKS 194)
haru tateba	Now that spring has come,
hana to ya mi*ramu*	*Does he* mistake them for flowers—
shirayuki no	That warbler singing
kakareru eda ni	Among the branches laden
uguisu no naku	With drifts of snowy white flakes?
	(KKS 6)

21

> hisakata no
> hikari nodokeki
> haru no hi ni
> shizugokoro naku
> hana no chiru*ramu*

> On this springtime day
> When the celestial orb
> Diffuses mild light,
> *Why should* the cherry blossoms
> Scatter with unquiet hearts?

(KKS 84)

c. *Ramu* occasionally indicates conjecture about habit or regular occurrence.

Example:
> Ōmu ito aware nari; hito no iu*ramu* koto o manebu*ramu* yo: The parrot is most delightful; it seems to make a habit of repeating what people say. (*Mak.*)

d. In *rentaikei* position, *ramu*, like *meri*, may be simply a softening device.

Example:
> Aga hotoke, nanigoto omoitamau zo. Obosu*ran* koto nanigoto zo: What are you thinking about, my darling? What *might be* troubling you? (*Take.*)

5. *Nari* (incomplete *rahen*: —/ —/ nari/ naru/ nare/ —/)
When *nari* follows the *shūshikei*, it either (1) indicates that the speaker is reporting hearsay evidence or (2), like *rashi*, signals a conclusion drawn on the basis of objective evidence. These two uses are restricted to Heian and Heian-style works. (Do not confuse with the more common *nari* that follows the *rentaikei* and substantives, discussed under Suffixes Attached to the Rentaikei.) Note that the *ren'yōkei* does not occur.

a. The hearsay (*denbun* 伝聞) use. MJ: *sō da; no uwasa da; to ka iu.* English: "people say," "I hear."

Example:
> Kono jūgonichi ni nan, tsuki no miyako yori, Kaguyahime no mukae ni mōdeku*naru*: *I am told that* people are coming from the Moon Palace on the Fifteenth to fetch Kaguyahime. (*Take.*)

b. The inference (*suitei* 推定) use. This use is almost always linked to auditory evidence. MJ: *no yō da; rashii.* English: "It seems that."

Examples:
> Shizumarinu*nari*: [Everything is quiet now;] *it seems* that they have gone to bed. (*Genji*)
> Akikaze ni hatsukari ga ne zo kikoyu*naru*: *I seem to* hear the cry of a wild goose on the autumn wind. (KKS 207)

6. The negative suffix of conjecture *maji*
(shiku-type adjective: majikara/ majiku, majikari/ [mashiji], maji/ [mashijiki], majiki/ majikere/ —/)

Maji has the same range of meanings as *beshi*, of which it is the negative counterpart. There is virtually no difference in meaning between *maji* and *bekarazu*. The difference between *ji* and *maji* corresponds to that between *mu* and *beshi*. *Maji* does not occur in poetry.

Meanings:

a. Simple negative conjecture. MJ: *mai*.

Example:
Fuyugare no keshiki koso, aki ni wa otoru*majikere*: A withered winter scene, we can *probably* say, is *not* inferior to autumn. (TZG)

b. Negative conjecture based on circumstance or reason. MJ: *nai ni chigai-nai*.

Example:
Yuku sora mo oboesōrau*maji*: [I will be so distraught that] I will *certainly not* even be conscious of my surroundings as I travel. (*Heiji monogatari*)

c. Negative conjecture about what is natural, fitting, or proper. MJ: *hazu ga nai, wake ga arumai; tekitō de nai darō; -te wa warukarō, -te wa ikenai.* English: "[probably] ought not." Within this general context, *maji* sometimes functions as a direct or indirect prohibition.

Examples:
Kakute miyako e yuku ni, Shimasaka nite hitoaruji shitari. Kanarazu shi mo aru*majiki* waza nari: While we were thus going toward the capital, a stranger entertained us at Shimasaka. It was a gesture that was *not necessarily appropriate.* (*Tosa*)
Shisasu*majiki* koto: Things that ought not to be left unfinished. (*Mak.*)
Sore ni mo uchitoketamau*maji*: It won't do for you to be off your guard, either. (*Heike*)

d. Negative desire or intention. MJ: *nai tsumori da; ki wa nai; mai.*

Example:
Tadaima wa miru*maji* tote irinu to Tonomozukasa ga iishikaba: Since the messenger from the Bureau of Grounds said, "She went to her room, saying, '*I don't feel like* looking at it now'" . . . (*Mak.*)

e. Conjectured impossibility. MJ: *dekinai darō; dekimai.*

Example:
Kono onna mide wa, yo ni aru*majiki* kokochi no shikereba: Since he felt that he *could not* go on living unless he married this woman . . . (*Take.*)

23

SUFFIXES ATTACHED TO THE RENTAIKEI

Note: The *rentaikei* will sometimes be found alone in final position without a preceding *ya, ka, namu,* or *zo.* Such substitution for the *shūshikei,* a phenomenon called *rentaidome* 連体止め, becomes increasing common after the beginning of the Kamakura period. When *rentaidome* occurs in a Heian text, it is said to add emphasis, suggesting a following *koso nare* (MJ: *koto desu yo*).

There are two common *rentaikei* suffixes, *gotoshi* and *nari.*

1. The comparison suffix (*hikyō no jodōshi* 比況の助動詞) gotoshi. (incomplete ku-type adjective: —/ gotoku/ gotoshi/ gotoki/ —/ —/)
   Gotoshi derives from the noun *koto* plus the adjective-forming *shi.* It expresses likeness or identity. Always with the same basic meaning, it may follow:
   a. The *rentaikei* plus *ga* or *no*

   > Example:
   > Hōun hōshi no sekishitsu o miru ga *gotoshi*: *It was like* seeing the monk Hōun's stone chamber. (*Oku no hosomichi*)

   b. The *rentaikei* directly

   > Example:
   > Hana no chirinishi *gotoki* wa ga ōkimi ka mo: Alas for my great lord, who is *like* the scattered blossoms! (MYS 477)

   c. A substantive plus *ga* or *no*

   > Example:
   > Ogoreru hito mo hisashikarazu, tada haru no yo no yume no *gotoshi:* The proud ones, too, endure but for a moment; they are *like* a dream on a spring night. (*Heike*)

   d. A substantive directly (post-Heian)

   > Example:
   > Kotsujiki junrei *gotoki* no hito: People *resembling* mendicant monks on a pious pilgrimage. (*Oku no hosomichi*. The insertion of *no* between *gotoki* and the word being modified was not uncommon in Bashō's day.)

Note: During the Nara and Heian periods, the stem *goto* was sometimes used as an alternative to the *ren'yōkei gotoku*.

Example:

ashihiki no	Do you, o cuckoo
yamahototogisu	From the foot-wearing hills,
waga *goto* ya	Seek in vain to sleep,
kimi ni koitsutsu	Your heart, *like* mine, never free
inekate ni suru	Of longing for a loved one?

(KKS 499)

2. The designation (*shitei* 指定) or predication (*dantei* 断定) suffix nari. (incomplete *rahen*: nara/ nari, ni/ nari/ naru/ nare/ —/)

This suffix, equivalent to MJ *de aru* or *da*, follows the *rentaikei*, a substantive, or an uninflected adjective. It occurs in works of all periods. Do not confuse with the special Heian hearsay or inference *nari*, which follows the *shūshikei*. (The difference in meaning between a sentence ending in the *rentaikei* plus *nari* and a similar sentence without *nari* is relatively slight, but the former explains or describes a situation, or asks a question about a situation, whereas the latter simply makes a statement or asks a question. This *nari* may be rendered in English as "the fact is," "the situation is," etc., but is usually better untranslated.)

Examples:

Ureshiki hitodomo *nari*: You are happy men. (*Take.*)

Kiyoge *naru* ya: Attractive-looking buildings. (*Genji*)

Kirime o mite tsukōmatsurubeki *nari*: [The fact is that] people ought to take the occasion into consideration when they compose poetry. (*Ōkagami*)

Onna mo shite mimu tote suru *nari*: A woman, too, will try her hand at it. (*Tosa*)

Notes:

1. The *shitei nari* sometimes indicates location. In such cases, it usually occurs in its *rentaikei* form.

Examples:

Ise no kuni *narikeru* onna: A woman who was *in* Ise Province. (*Ise*)

Sato *naru* saburai meshi ni tsukawashi nado su: We sent people to summon the attendants who were *at* home. (*Mak.*)

2. In Tokugawa and later works, the *rentaikei* of the *shitei nari* may appear as an equivalent of *to iu* (be called).

Example:

Shigeatsu *naru* hito: A man *called* Shigeatsu.

SUFFIXES ATTACHED TO THE IZENKEI

Note: In poetry, and also in Nara-period prose, the *izenkei* sometimes occurs alone or with the dubitative/interrogative particle *ya*. When it is alone, it means "because." When followed by *ya*, it indicates (1) a rhetorical question, (2) speculation about cause, or (3) simple speculation.

Example:
> Naniwa no haru wa yume *nare ya*: Was it a dream—that springtime in Naniwa? (*Shinkokinshū* 625)

As in modern Japanese, the principal *izenkei* suffixes are *do/domo* and *ba*.

1. *Do* and *Domo* (uninflected; classified as conjunctive particles)

Do and *domo*, which can be regarded as identical in meaning, are concessive conjunctive particles used between two contrasting statements of fact (or, rarely, to indicate a hypothetical concession). MJ: *ga; keredomo; mo; -te mo; tatte*. English: "even though," "but." Do not confuse with the pluralizing suffix *domo*, which follows substantives—e.g. *hitodomo*, people.

Examples:
> Soko ni ari to kike*do*: *Although* he had heard that she was in a certain place . . . (*Ise*)
> Fumi o kakite yare*do*, kaerigoto sezu: *Although* they wrote letters and sent them, she did not answer. (*Take*.)
> Sono nochi hisashū miene*do*, tare ka wa omoiiden: *Although* she failed to appear for a long time afterward, who gave her a thought? [Nobody.] (*Mak.*)

Note: In texts of the twelfth century and the medieval period, the phrase *to iedomo* is often identical in meaning with *do/domo*.

Example:
> Kurushi *to iedomo*, uma, ushi, kuruma to kokoro o nayamasu ni wa shikazu: *Although* [walking] is arduous, it is better than bothering with horses, oxen, and carriages. (*Hōjōki*)

2. *Ba* (uninflected; classified as a conjunctive particle)

In literary Japanese, the suffix *ba*, which follows the *izenkei* in modern Japanese, may follow either the *izenkei* or the *mizenkei*. Its meanings vary accordingly.

a. Common uses after the *izenkei*

When *ba* follows the *izenkei*, it usually indicates that the preceding sequence is the condition under which the following sequence occurs.

(1) Most frequently, the preceding sequence is a cause of, or reason for, the following sequence. MJ: *no de; kara.* English: "because," "since."

Examples:
> Moto yori tsumako nakere*ba*, sutegataki yosuga mo nashi: *Since* I had never had a wife and children, there was no one close to me whom it would be difficult to leave. (*Hōjōki*)
> Sore ga saburawane*ba* koso, torimōshitsure: I ask for this precisely *because* I lack that. (*Mak.*)
> On-tsukai ni Tadataka mairitare*ba*, shitone sashiidashite mono nado iu: Tadataka came with a message from the Emperor, *so* we put out a cushion and chatted with him. (*Mak.*)

(2) The preceding sequence may be a temporal condition for the following sequence. MJ: *to; -tara.* English: "when," "upon."

Examples:
> yamazakura   *When* I came to see
> wa ga mi ni kure*ba*   The mountain cherry blossoms,
> harugasumi   Springtime veils of haze,
> mine ni mo o ni mo   Hovering on peaks and slopes,
> tachikakushitsutsu   Concealed them from my eyes.
> (KKS 51)
> Onokodomo mese*ba*, kurōdo Tadataka Narinaka mairitareba: *When* they summoned attendants, the Chamberlains Tadataka and Narinaka came . . . (*Mak.*)

(3) The preceding sequence may be a regular condition of the following sequence. MJ: *to; itsu mo; toki kanarazu.* English: "whenever."

Examples:
> Inochi nagakere*ba* haji ōshi: *Whenever* life is long, there is much shame. (TZG)
> Ōja akirakaran to sure*ba*, zanshin kore o kurō su: *Whenever* a ruler seeks the light, a lying minister spreads darkness. (*Heike*)

b. Less common uses of *ba*

(1) *Ba* may sometimes be used to contrast a preceding statement with a following one.

Example:
> Kabura wa umi e irikere*ba*, ōgi wa sora e zo agarikeru: The

humming-bulb arrow went into the sea; the fan flew up toward the heavens. (*Heike*)

(2) When *ba* follows the *izenkei ne* of the negative suffix *zu*, it can mean *nai no ni* (although . . . not). The form is often preceded by *mo*. (Chiefly Heian and earlier texts)

Example:
Wa ga niwa no hagi no shitaba wa akikaze mo imada fukane*ba*, kaku zo momideru: *Although* the autumn wind has *not* yet blown on the lower leaves of the bush-clover in my garden, how brilliantly they are colored! (MYS)

(3) *Ba* may occasionally mean *no ni* (although).

Example:
Iro ni wa mo ideji to omoe*ba*, koto no shigekeku: *Although* I have been determined not to show [my love] in my behavior. rumors are flying thick and fast. (MYS)

THE "MEIREIKEI" SUFFIX RI

The *rahen* suffix *ri* can be thought of as following the *meireikei* of *yodan* and *sahen* verbs and suffixes. (It does not ordinarily occur with verbs or suffixes belonging to other categories.) It originated when the initial *a* of *ari* combined with the final vowel of a preceding *ren'yōkei* to produce *eri* (thus *yomeri* from *yomi ari, kakeri* from *kaki ari*), a form resembling either an *izenkei* or a *meireikei* plus *ri*. In committing the form to writing, the *Man'yōshū* editors, who regularly preserved a distinction between the *izenkei* and the *meireikei*, attached *ri* to the *meireikei*. It is solely for this reason that *ri* is said to follow the *meireikei*. The meanings of *ri* are the same as those of the *ren'yōkei* suffix tari:

1. Completion of an act or process. MJ: *-ta*. English: past tense.

> Example:
> Mina zō taen koto o negaitamae*ri*: They all ask*ed* for their descendants to die out. (TZG)

2. Continuation of the result of a completed act or state. MJ: *-te iru; -te aru; -ta; -ta koto ga aru*. English: past, perfect, or past perfect tense.

> Examples:
> | | |
> |---|---|
> | asaborake | In dawn's first dim light |
> | ariake no tsuki to | We almost mistake them for |
> | miru made ni | Pale morning moonbeams— |
> | Yoshino-no-sato ni | The snowflakes that *have fallen* |
> | fure*ru* shirayuki | At Yoshino-no-sato. (KKS 332) |
>
> Yotsugi no okina no monogatari ni wa ie*ri*: It *is said* in *The Tale of Old Yotsugi*. (TZG)

3. Continuation of an act or state. MJ: *-te iru; -te aru*. English: progressive or imperfect tense.

> Examples:
> Tsuki no katabuku made, fuse*rite*: He *continued to* lie there until the moon sank low . . . (*Ise*)
> | | |
> |---|---|
> | kirigirisu | Do not wail, crickets, |
> | itaku na naki so | In such despairing accents. |
> | aki no yo no | Though your sorrows be |
> | nagaki omoi wa | Longlasting as autumn nights, |
> | ware zo masare*ru* | My own woes *are longer still*. |
> | | (KKS 196) |

IMPORTANT PARTICLES AND MISCELLANEOUS PARTS OF SPEECH

Particles play an important role in literary texts. Some need no particular explanation. Of the others, the most significant are discussed in alphabetical order below, together with a few other miscellaneous expressions. The student should also remember that *kobun* sometimes omits particles where MJ would supply them, particularly after subjects and objects.

1. Omission of particle after subject

The subject of an inflected word may occur without a particle to mark it. See *Ga*.

Examples:
Yanagi ōku ari: There are many willow trees.
Kaze fuku: The wind blows.
Namida otsu: Tears fall.

2. Omission of particle after object

The direct object of a verb may occur without a particle to mark it. See also *O*.

Examples:
Kuruma yosete: Bringing up the carriage.
Momiji mite: Looking at autumn leaves.

Aku

Aku, an obsolete noun meaning *koto* or *tokoro*, combines with a preceding *rentaikei* to produce a substantive. Sound changes result in forms resembling (1) the *mizenkei* plus *ku* (for *yodan* and *rahen* verbs and suffixes), (2) the *shūshikei* plus *raku* (for *kahen*, *sahen*, *nahen*, *kami nidan*, and *shimo nidan*), or (3) the *mizenkei* or *ren'yōkei* plus *raku* (for *kami ichidan*).

Examples:
Verbs: iwa*ku* (*yodan*), ara*ku* (*rahen*)
ku*raku* (*kahen*), su*raku* (*sahen*), shinu*raku* (*nahen*), otsu*raku* (*kami nidan*), fu*raku* (*shimo nidan*)
mi*raku* (*kami ichidan*)
Adjectives: samuk*eku*, suzushik*eku*

Suffixes: mima*ku*
For the *kanryō* suffix *ki*, the form is *shiku* (e.g. yomi*shiku*, mi*shiku*)

The most common use of the form is to introduce a quotation.

Example:
Miko kotaete notamawa*ku*: What the prince said in reply [was this]. (*Take.*)

Ba (particle) For uses with *mizenkei* and *izenkei*, see pp. 6 and 26. See also **O Ba** below.

Bakari (adverbial particle) Follows substantives, *rentaikei* (rarely, *shūshikei*), adverbs, particles, etc.

1. Limitation. Singles out one thing from an actual or potential group. MJ: *dake*. English: "only."

Examples:

isonokami	*Only* the singing
furuki miyako no	Of the cuckoo has survived
hototogisu	Here at the ancient
koe *bakari* koso	Isonokami capital
mukashi narikere	Long fallen into ruins. (KKS 144)

Sarubeki hi *bakari* mōde: Visiting it *only* on the designated days . . . (TZG)

2. Extent, range

a. Degree. MJ: *hodo*. English: "as . . . as."

Examples:
Once a man spent a single night at a lady's house and then did not go there again. The lady took the lid from the tub where she washed her hands, gazed at her reflection in the water, and recited to herself:

ware *bakari*	No one else,
mono omou hito wa	I had thought,
mata mo araji	Could be *so* miserable *as* I—
to omoeba mizu no	Yet there is another
shita ni mo arikeri	Under the water. (*Ise*)

Hito no nakiato *bakari* kanashiki wa nashi: There is nothing *as* sad *as* the time after someone's death. (TZG)

b. Quantity. MJ: *gurai*. English: "about."

Example:
Nijūnin *bakari* ni narinikeri: [The number] reached *about* twenty people. (*Mak.*)

c. Time. MJ: *koro, goro*. English, "around," "about."

Example:
Yayoi *bakari* ni: *Around* the Third Month. (*Ise*)

d. Place

Example:
Yama no anata *bakari* ni: *Somewhere* beyond the hill.
(Kagerō nikki)

3. Extreme degree. MJ: *hodo ni mo*; (with negative) *gurai. . . nai*

Examples:
Shinden no on-shitsurai . . . kagayaku *bakari* shitamaite: He provided furnishings for the main residence which were *so* splendid *as to* glitter. *(Genji)*
Kin nado mo tenjin oru *bakari* hikite: He played the zither *so extremely* well *that* heavenly beings descended. *(Mak.)*

Baya, *see* p. 5

Dani

The adverbial particles (*fukujoshi* 副助詞) *dani, sura,* and *sae* can all be translated "even." Their meanings, however, are not quite identical. In Heian texts, *dani* and *sura* correspond to MJ *sae; sae,* to MJ *made mo. Dani* and *sura* resemble one another so closely that Heian writers seem to have felt little need to use *sura,* which rarely appears except in poetry. The fine distinction between the two is that *dani,* in pointing to a lower limit, minimum degree, or lesser importance, indirectly suggests the remainder, the larger degree, or the greater importance, while, *sura,* in pointing to A, emphasizes the fact that the same holds for B.

Examples:
Sore o *dani* keyakeki koto ni omoitamaeshi ni: Although *even* that [relatively unimpressive performance] seemed superb to me . . . *(Ōkagami)*
Na o *dani* shirazu: They don't *even* know his name [much less anything else about him]. (TZG)
Hito *dani* mireba usenu: It disappears whenever anyone *so much as* looks at it. *(Take.)*
Ware ya wa hana ni te *dani* furetaru: Have I *so much as* ventured to lay a hand on the flowers? (KKS 106)
Yoso nite kikitsuru *dani,* kashira no ke futorite osoroshiki ni, mashite sono ie e yukamu . . . : *Even* to hear about him made people's hair stand on end—to say nothing of going to his house . . . *(Konjaku monogatari)*
Koto towanu ki *sura*: Even the trees, which lack the gift of speech [and certainly I, too] . . . (MYS)

Note: *Dani* is often associated with imperatives, and with expressions of desire, hope, etc. It can then usually be translated "at least." MJ: *semete. . . dake*

Examples:
> Ima *dani* nanori shitamae: *At least* tell me your name now. (*Genji*)
> Chirinu tomo ka o *dani* nokose ume no hana: Even if you fall, *at least* leave
> your scent, plum blossoms. (KKS 48)

Sae is used when the speaker, after naming A, wishes to indicate that B is to be
added to it. MJ: *made mo*. English: "even [on top of that]."

Example:
> Tada namida ni hijite akashi-kurasasetamaeba, mitatematsuru hito *sae* tsu-
> yukeki aki nari: Since he lived with his sleeves constantly drenched with
> tears, that damp autumn was one in which *even* those who saw him felt
> gloomy. [Not only the emperor, but also his attendants . . .] (*Genji*)

De

The instrumental or locative particle *de* does not appear before the Kamakura period. It is thought to derive from *nite*. For the copular *de*, see **Nite**;
for *de* as a suffix to the *mizenkei*, see p. 8.

Ga

Ga may appear in literary texts as a case, conjunctive, or final particle. In
eleventh-century and earlier texts, it occurs frequently as a case particle,
occasionally as a final particle, and probably never as a conjunctive particle. In all periods, its principal case-particle uses resemble those of *no*
(which see): either *ga* or *no* can make a clause modify a substantive, and
either can mark the subject of an inflected word. Since the original and fun-
damental use of both *ga* and *no* appears to have been to form modifying
clauses, the usual rule is that when one of them functions as a nominative
particle it marks the subject of a subordinate clause. *Bungo* therefore differs
from MJ in that *ga* does not ordinarily appear after the subject of the main
predicate.

> Taketori no okina to iu mono arikeri: There was someone called the
> old bamboo-cutter. (*Take.*)

1. Case-particle uses
   As a case particle, *ga* follows substantives (including *rentaikei* substantives).
   a. Attributive case
      Ga may indicate an attributive relationship between a preceding word
      and a following substantive. MJ: *no*
      (1) Between two substantives, *ga* may indicate:
          (a) Possession
              > Shirome *ga* uta nari: It is Shirome's poem. (*Ōkagami*)
          (b) Affiliation, attachment
              > Kami *ga* kami wa, uchiokihaberinu: I have set aside the
              > highest *of the* high. (*Genji*)

(c) Apposition

Mikka *ga* [= to iu] hodo wa, yogarenaku wataritamau o:
Since he went every night for a period [*consisting*] of
three days. . . (*Genji*)

(2) A redundant *ga* may appear between a *rentaikei* and a substantive.

nuru *ga* uchi ni	Why should we say "dream"
miru o nomi ya wa	Only of that which we see
yume to iwamu	While we lie asleep?
hakanaki yo o mo	This fugitive world itself
utsutsu to wa mizu	Is scarcely reality. (KKS 835)

Note: When the attributive case particle *ga* is preceded, but not followed, by a substantive, it may function as a quasi-substantive.

Kono uta wa, aru hito, Ariwara no Tokiharu *ga* [saku] to mo iu:
Some people say that this poem is [a composition] of Ariwara
no Tokiharu. (KKS 355)

b. Nominative case

Ga may indicate the subject of a predicate

(1) Between a substantive and a predicate. MJ: *ga* or *no*.

Kaneyuki *ga* kakeru tobira, azayaka ni miyuru zo aware naru:
How moving it is that Kaneyuki's writing on the door should
still be plainly visible. (TZG).

Kono yamamori *ga* oru tokoro nari: It is the place where this
mountain guardian lives. (*Hōjōki*)

(2) Between a *rentaikei* and a predicate. MJ: *no ga; koto ga.* (There
is no parallel use of *no*.) Note that this *ga* us not a conjunctive
particle.

Mizudori no hima naku ite tachisawagishi *ga* ito okashū mieshi
nari: The great flocks of noisy waterfowl made an extremely
interesting spectacle. (*Mak.*)

Note: Some scholars list a "complementary case" (*hokaku* 補格) to account
for the use of *ga* as a "complementary word" before *gotoshi, yō nari,
manimani, muta,* and similar expressions. For an example with
gotoshi, see p. 24.

2. Conjunctive-particle uses (twelfth century and later)

As a conjunctive particle, *ga* follows the *rentaikei*. It has two uses.

a. Concessive. MJ: *keredomo.*

Mukashi yori ōku no shirabyōshi arishi *ga,* kakaru mai wa imada
mizu: Since ancient times there have been many shirabyōshi
[dancers], *but* we have never before seen such dancing. (*Heike*)

b. Simple conjunction indicating a vague relationship between two
clauses.

MJ: *ga.* English: "and"; semicolon.

Kiso wa Echigo no kokufu ni arikeru *ga* kore o kiite gomanki de hasemukau: Kiso was in the Echigo provincial seat, *and* when he heard this he galloped toward [the enemy] with 50,000 horsemen.

(*Heike*)

3. Final-particle use

Ga functions as a desiderative in such final-particle combinations as *ga na, mo ga, mo ga na*, and *mo ga mo*. For examples, see **Ga Na**.

Gachi (Classified as a suffix [*setsubi* 接尾])

Gachi may occur after a substantive, the *ren'yōkei* of a verb, the *rentaikei* of an adjective, etc. It indicates likelihood, tendency, or periodic or frequent occurrence.

Examples:
Sode nure*gachi* nari: Their sleeves were always being dampened. (*Genji*)
Kumori*gachi* ni haberumeri: It seems to be clouding over. (*Genji*)

Ga Na

a. Desiderative use

When *ga na* appears at the end of a sentence, it functions as a desiderative combination of particles. It is almost always preceded by the emphatic particle *mo* or the emphatic particle *shi*, the latter of which in turn is usually preceded by the particle *te*. *Mo* may replace *na* or appear between *ga* and *na*; *ga* may appear alone. Of the various combinations thus produced, the most common are *ga na, shi ga, shi ga na, mo ga na, mo ga mo na*, and *te shi ga na*. Any of them may follow almost any part of speech.

Examples:
Oizu shinazu no kusuri *mo ga*: *Would that* I possessed the elixir of immortality. (KKS 1003)
Aware, momiji o takan hito *mo ga na*: Ah! *If only* there were someone to burn leaves. (TZG)
Sate mo saburai*te shi ga na* to omoedo: Although he would have *dearly loved* to stay longer . . . (*Ise*)

b. Indefinite expression, usually of desire or intent (chiefly medieval)

In medial position, the phrase *ga na* and its variants indicate vagueness or uncertainty on the part of the speaker, usually connected with desire or intent.

Example:
Nani o *ga na* katami ni ōna ni torasemu: Let me see . . . I want to give the old woman something as a keepsake. (*Konjaku monogatari*)
MJ: *ēto, nani ka* . . .

Garu (classified as a suffix [*setsubi* 接尾])

When added to a noun or adjective stem, *garu* forms a *yodan* verb expressing desire, opinion, feeling, apparent feeling, giving or trying to give the appearance of, etc. English: "feel," "want," "seem," etc.

Examples:
>Medeta*garite*: *Considering* it splendid . . . *(Ōkagami)*
>Tsuki o aware*garit*amaedo: Although she has always *seemed* to be deeply moved by the moon . . . *(Take.)*

Ge (classified as a suffix [*setsubi* 接尾])

Ge follows substantives, adjective stems, the *ren'yōkei* of verbs, etc. It indicates external conjecture about situation, feeling, tendency, etc.
MJ: *no yōsu; -sō*

Example:
>Katachi okashi*ge* nareba: Since her face was attractive-*looking* . . .
>*(Ōkagami)*

Hodo

The noun *hodo* has a number of sometimes confusing uses stemming from its basic meaning of "amount," "extent," "so much," "as much."
1. Temporal uses
>a. Temporal interval, period of time. MJ: *aida, uchi, jikan, tsukihi, toshitsuki*

>Examples:
>>Sono *hodo* mo, kore ga ushirometakereba: I was anxious about this *during that period*, too, and so. . . . *(Mak.)*
>>Mitoshi ga *hodo* ni arehatete: They fell into ruin in *the course of* three years . . . *(Heike)*
>>*Hodo* hete: Time passed . . . *(Ise)*

>Note: *Hodo nashi* means "with no elapsed time," "immediately."
>MJ: *ma mo naku*

>Example:
>>*Hodo naku* sotoba mo koke mushi: *In no time*, moss grows on the grave marker . . . (TZG)

>b. Time, occasion, season. MJ: *ori, koro, jibun, kisetsu*

>Examples:
>>Mishi *hodo* o omoiyaru mo okashi: It was amusing to recall the *occasion* on which they had seen her. *(Genji)*
>>Hatsuka no *hodo* ni ame furedo: Although rain fell *around* the Twentieth . . . *(Mak.)*

>c. Time of life; age

Examples:

Ito warinaki on-*hodo*: A quite unsuitable age [for marriage]. (*Genji*)
Nagaku tomo yosoji ni taranu *hodo* nite shinamu koso meyasukaru-bekere. Sono *hodo* suginureba: It must be considered desirable to die at an *age* before forty, at the latest. Once anybody passes that *age* . . . (TZG)

2. Spatial uses

a. Distance, spatial interval. MJ: *kyori, hedatari*

Example:

Sukoshi *hodo* tōki kokochi suru ni: He had rather the feeling that the distance was considerable, but . . . (*Genji*)

b. Width, area. MJ: *hirosa, menseki*

Example:

Sono chi *hodo* sebakute jōri o waru ni tarazu: The *area* of the site was so cramped that there was not enough room to divide it into [the proper number of] streets. (*Hōjōki*)

c. Length, dimensions, measurements. MJ: *nagasa, sunpō*

Example:

Kyō no *hodo* o hakarite [kyōbako o] tsukurashimu: He had him measure the *dimensions* of the sutra and make [a box for it]. (*Nihon ryōiki*)

d. Depth (usually figurative). MJ: *fukasa*

Example:

Nani ka kurikaeshi-kikoeshirasuru kokoro no *hodo* o tsutsumitamau-ramu: Why are you reluctant to recognize the *depth* of the feelings I have expressed? (*Genji*)

e. Vicinity, area nearby. MJ: *atari*

Example:

Tsuiji no *hodo* ni hisashi shite itaru o . . . yobiyosete: I called over a man who had made himself an eave-shelter *near* the wall . . .
(*Mak.*)

3. Miscellaneous uses

a. Amount, extent, degree. MJ: *teido, hodoai*

Example:

Warōda no *hodo* nan haberi: There is *an amount the size of* a cushion.
(*Mak.*)

b. Condition, state. MJ: *guai, anbai, yōsu, chōshi, arisama*

Examples:
>Mochizuki no kuma naki o . . . nagametaru yori mo . . . [tsuki wa] uchishiguretaru murakumogakure no *hodo* mata naku aware nari: Superior to the full moon seen in a cloudless sky is the incomparable charm of the *spectacle* [the moon presents] as it hides behind masses of clouds during a shower. (TZG)
>On-kaeshi kakasetamau *hodo* mo, ito medetashi: The *manner* in which Her Majesty wrote the reply was also very splendid.
>*(Mak.)*
>Mono kazuketamau *hodo* no koto . . . kuwashiku zo kataru: He described in detail how they gave her presents. *(Ōkagami)*

c. Social status. MJ: *mibun, iegara, chii*

Example:
>Onaji *hodo* sore yori gerō no kōitachi: Concubines who were of the same or lower *status. (Genji)*

Note: In post-Heian texts, *hodo* may also occur as a particle meaning "when," "while," "because," "degree," "extent."

Ji, *see* p. 8

Ka

As a particle, *ka* may be either interrogative or interjectional. See also **Ya.**

a. Interrogative use

(1) In medial position

>*Ka* may occur medially in sentences with interrogative words such as *nani, izure*, etc. It indicates interrogation, a rhetorical question, or doubt. The final inflected form in the sentence will ordinarily be a *rentaikei*. (See Kakarimusubi and Other Grammatical Patterns.)
>MJ: sentence-final *ka* or *darō ka*

Examples:
>Nan no utagai *ka* aramu: What doubt can there be? [None.]
>*(Take.)*
>Ika naru kokorozashi aramu hito ni *ka* awamu to obosu: What kind of sentiments do you require in the person you would marry? *(Take.)*
>Kakaru michi ni wa, ika de *ka* owasuru: What are you doing on a road like this? *(Ise)*

(2) In final position

>When *ka* occurs in sentence-final position after a substantive, it may function as a tentative interrogative copular.
>MJ: *darō ka*

Examples:
> Yume *ka*: Was it *perhaps* a dream? (KKS)
> Mai nado suru *ka*: Do you dance, *by any chance*? (*Mak.*)

b. Interjectional use

The interjectional *ka* occurs in final position after substantives and the *rentaikei.*

Examples:
> Ureshiku mo aru *ka*: Ah, what happiness! (MYS)
> Wari naku mo nete mo samete mo koishiki *ka*: Waking and sleeping, I am held fast in the toils of this sad yearning! (KKS 570)

Ka Na

Ka na, an exclamatory combination of particles, appears in sentence-final position. It often, but not always, indicates sad emotion. See also **Na.**

Example:
> Obotsukanaku mo yobukodori *ka na*: How uneasily I listen to a questing bird's plaintive call! (KKS 29)

Ka Shi

Ka shi, an exclamatory combination of particles, appears most often in final position.

Example:
> Mitsune ga bechiroku tamawaru ni tatoshie naki utayomi nari *ka shi*: He was a poet who *certainly* could not compare with Mitsune, who received a special reward. (*Ōkagami*)

Keku, *see* Aku

Kerashi   This form is a contraction of *keru* (*rentaikei* of *keri*) plus *rashi.*

Koso

When a clause contains *koso*, its final inflected form will normally be the *izenkei.* (See Kakarimusubi and Other Grammatical Patterns.) The particle has the following uses.

1. Adverbial particle (follows substantives, adverbs, particles, etc.)

As an adverbial particle, *koso* indicates stronger emphasis than *zo* or *namu.*

a. In medial position (follows almost any part of speech)

When in medial position, *koso* indicates strong emphasis on a preceding word. It is often used when the word emphasized stands in contrast to, or is to be particularly distinguished from, something else. The meaning is perhaps best conveyed in English by the kind of stress sometimes represented by italics.

Examples:
> Kaerigoto ni iiatetarishi *koso*, ito okashikarishika: That you

should have guessed correctly in your answer—ah! *that* was most amusing. (*Mak.*)

Nowaki no ashita *koso* okashikere: The morning after a typhoon—ah, *that* is delightful. (TZG)

b. Before a final *izenkei* in a clause stating a fact, *koso* may function as a concessive particle.

Examples:

Mukashi *koso* yoso ni mo mishika, wagimoko ga okutsuki to omoeba hashiki Saoyama: In the past, Saoyama seemed no concern of mine, *but* now my wife's grave makes it dear to me. (MYS 474)

Nakagaki *koso* are, hitotsu ie no yō nareba, nozomite azukareru nari: There is, *to be sure,* a fence; *however,* [the two houses] resemble a single property, and so [the neighbors] volunteered to take care of [our place]. (*Tosa*)

c. In final position when a final inflected word has been omitted, *koso* indicates strong emphasis.

Examples:

Shimo ni aru hitobito no madoinoboru sama *koso* [imijikere]: The manner in which the ladies who had been in their private rooms rushed pellmell to [the Seiryōden] was indeed [something to behold]! (*Mak.*)

Gotokudaiji no otodo no shinden ni tobi isaseji tote, nawa o hararetarikeru o, Saigyō ga mite, "Tobi no itaramu nani ka wa kurushikarubeki. Kono tono no on-kokoro sabakari ni *koso* [arikere]" tote, sono nochi wa mairazarikeru to: The Later Tokudaiji Minister stretched a rope over his main building to keep the kites away. When Saigyō saw the rope, he said, "What harm would it do for kites to perch there? So that's the kind of heart this minister has!" People say he never went there afterward. (TZG)

d. When *koso* follows the *mizenkei*-plus-*ba* in a hypothetical statement about an unlikely situation, it negates the second element in the statement. "In the unlikely event that X were true, Y would certainly be the case; however, X is not true, and therefore Y will not be the case."

Example:

A ga omou imo mo	Were she but there—
Ari to iwaba *koso*	That girl who is in my thoughts—
Kuni ni mo	Then *indeed* would I go to my province
Ie ni mo yukame	And to my home . . . (MYS 3263)

e. When *koso* follows the *izenkei* with no intervening suffix (*jodōshi*), it indicates positive affirmation. (Pre-Heian)

Example:

yū sareba	*Just because* I know
kimi ni awamu	I shall meet you
to omoe *koso*	When night shadows fall,
hi no kururaku mo	The ending of the day
ureshikarikere	Has filled me with joy. (MYS 2922)

2. Final particle following *ren'yōkei* (pre-Heian)

As a final particle after the *ren'yōkei*, *koso* indicates a hope or demand directed by the speaker toward a person or thing other than himself. MJ: *shite moraitai, shite kure*

Example:

Asabiraki wa wa kogiidenu to ie ni tsuge *koso*: Tell them at home that I rowed out at break of day. (MYS 4408)

3. Vocative particle (Heian period)

When *koso* follows a personal name, it may function as a respectful vocative particle.

Example:

Ukon-no-kimi *koso*, mazu mitamae: "Ukon-no-kimi, come quickly and look." (*Genji*)

Ku, *see* **Aku**
Meku

The *yodan* suffix *meku*, which follows nouns and adverbs, means seem or resemble.

Example:

Yama no momiji iro o tsukushite mo kotosara*meki*: The infinite variety of colors in the autumn leaves on the hills also *seemed* purposely arranged . . . (*Eiga monogatari*)

Mi

The uninflected suffix *mi* appears most frequently in the two uses below.

1. Substantivizing use

When *mi* follows an adjective stem, the resultant form may function as a substantive.

Example:

Natsu no no no shige*mi*: The luxuriance of the summer fields. (MYS)

2. Indication of cause or reason

　　When *mi* follows the stem of an adjective or of an adjective-type suffix, it may indicate cause or reason. It is often preceded by the interjectional particle *o*. MJ: *no yue ni, ni yotte, na no de.*

Examples:

　　　Yama taka*mi* tsune ni arashi no fuku sato: A village where there are constant gales *because* the mountains are high. (KKS)

　　　Io no toma o ara*mi* waga koromode wa tsuyu ni nuretsutsu: *Because* the rush thatch on my cottage is coarse, my sleeves are drenched with dew. (*Gosenshū*)

Mo

The principal *bungo* uses of *mo* correspond generally to those of MJ. They may be categorized as follows.

1. Adverbial-particle use

　　As an adverbial particle, *mo* follows substantives, adverbs, verbs, other particles, etc. It adds emphasis, usually rather weak, to what precedes it. Some typical contexts are listed below.

　　a. In a statement of an extreme instance, *mo* indicates that the same is even more true of less extreme cases. MJ: *sae, datte.* English: "even."

Example:

　　　Waga on-ie e *mo* yoritamawazu shite owashimashitari: He has come without *even* stopping at his own house [much less anywhere else]. (*Take.*)

　　b. Strengthening meaning or adding an overtone of emotion

Example:

　　　E ni ito yoku *mo* nitaru ka na: It looks *just* like a picture!

(*Genji*)

　　c. Singling out of one of a number of similar things for comment

Example:

miyoshino no	Despite the cold
yama no arashi no	Of the mountain gale
samukeku ni	From fair Yoshino,
hata ya koyoi *mo*	Shall I sleep alone
a ga hitori nemu	*Again tonight*? (MYS 74)

　　d. Between two occurrences of the same verb, *mo* indicates extreme degree.

Example:

　　　Ware wa mono mo oboeneba, shiri *mo* shirarezu: Since I was

half unconscious, I understood nothing *at all*. (*Kagerō nikki*)

e. Enumeration of similar things

Example:
Kimi ga yo *mo* wa ga yo *mo* shiru ya: It governs *both* your life *and* mine. (MYS 10)

f. After an indefinite pronoun, *mo* acts as an inclusive particle.

Example:

sabishisa ni	Overcome by loneliness,
yado o tachiidete	I emerge from my dwelling
nagamureba	And look around me:
izuku *mo* onaji	It is the same *every*where—
aki no yūgure	The same autumnal twilight.
	(*Goshūishū* 333)

g. Indication of a correspondence between two or more things

Example:

yo no naka wa	So it is like this
kaku koso arikere	Between a man and a girl!
fuku kaze no [yō ni]	I yearn for someone
me ni minu hito *mo*	Heard of *as* we hear the wind,
koishikarikeri	And no more visible than it.
	(KKS 475)

h. Between a word meaning "very little" and a negative, *mo* means "[not] at all." MJ: *mattaku*

Example:
Saikō moto yori suguretaru daikō no mono narikereba, chitto *mo* iro mo hen sezu: Since Saikō was dauntless and brave by nature, he did not change color *at all*. (*Heike*)

2. Conjunctive-particle use

As a concessive conjunctive particle, *mo* occurs most frequently (but not exclusively) in post-Heian texts. It usually follows the *rentaikei* but may follow the *ren'yōkei*.

Example:
Kaerigoto mo sumaji to omou *mo*, "Ito nasake nashi. Amari nari," nado mono sureba: I was inclined not to answer, *but* [my attendants] said, "You are very cruel; it's too much," and so . . .
(*Kagerō nikki*)

3. Final-particle use

As a conclusive particle following the *shūshikei, mo* indicates emotion. MJ: *nā*. It appears only in MYS and in MYS-style Heian poems.

Example:

ashibe yori	What grief to see him
kumoi o sashite	Growing ever more remote—
yuku kari no	As when a wild goose
iya tōzakaru	Takes leave of the reedy shore
wa ga mi kanashi *mo*	And wings its way toward the sky.

(KKS 819)

Mo Ga Na, *see* Ga Na
Mo Koso, Mo Zo

Mo koso and *mo zo* are combinations of emphatic particles, virtually identical in meaning. They indicate either active worry or nervous speculation about the future. MJ: *ka mo shirenai, shi ya shinai kashira*. English: "I'm afraid that." The usual *kakarimusubi* rules apply (p. 71).

Examples:

Izukata e makarinuru . . . karasu nado *mo koso* mitsukure: Where have [the pet sparrows] gone? *I hope* the crows *don't* find them. (Genji)

Ame *mo zo* furu: *I'm afraid* it may rain. (TZG)

Mata ōserarekakubeki koto *mo zo* haberu; makaritachihaberinamu: *I'm afraid* there may be something else for you to tax me with, [so] I will leave. (*Mak.*)

Mono Ka and its Variant Mon Ka

Mono ka, a final combination of particles, follows the *rentaikei*. It may indicate:

a. An emphatic rhetorical question, stronger than *ka* alone

Example:

Hajime yori nagaku iitsutsu tanomezu wa kakaru omoi ni awamashi *mono ka*: Could I *possibly* have known such misery if you had not won my trust from the start with your talk of eternal fidelity? (MYS 620)

b. Strong emotion

Example:

Kata ni uchiokite wa mau *mono ka*: She *had the nerve to* put it on her shoulder and perform a dance! (*Mak.*)

Note: The addition of a final *wa* or *na* makes *mono ka* even more emphatic.

Examples:

Hana wa sakari ni tsuki wa kuma naki o nomi miru *mono ka wa*:

> Ought we to look at cherry blossoms only when they are at their best, or at the moon only when it is unclouded? [Certainly not.]
> (TZG)
> Imijikarishi *mono ka na*: How *very, very* splendid it was! (*Ōkagami*)

Mono Kara, Mono Yue [Ni]

Mono kara and *mono yue* [*ni*] can be regarded as interchangeable. They follow the *rentaikei*.

a. For Heian texts, the basic rule is that both *mono kara* and *mono yue* [*ni*] function as concessive combinations of particles. *Mono kara* is said to correspond to MJ *keredomo; mono yue*, to MJ *no ni*.

Examples:

matsu hito ni	First of the wild geese:
aranu *mono kara*	*Though* it is not the person
hatsukari no	I have waited for,
kesa naku koe no	How novel it is to hear
mezurashiki ka na	The calling voice this morning!
	(KKS 206)
aki narade	*Though* they do not grow
au koto kataki	[Solely] on the beaches alongside
ominaeshi	The heavenly stream,
ama no kawara ni	We cannot meet maidenflowers
oinu *mono yue*	Unless it be autumn. (KKS 231)

b. Particularly, but not only, in texts of the Edo period, these particles may sometimes mean "and," "and so," "because."

Example:

> Hendo no ifu wasurezaru *mono kara* shushō ni ooboeraru: I found [the songs] splendid *because* [the singer] had not forgotten the art that still lived in this remote place. (*Oku no hosomichi*)

Mono No, *see* Mono O

Mono O

Mono o occurs as a concessive conjunctive phrase and as an exclamatory final phrase. In both cases, it usually suggests regret, reluctance, dissatisfaction, disappointment, dejection, etc. It follows the *rentaikei*.

a. As a concessive conjunctive phrase

MJ: *de wa aru keredomo, no da ga, da no ni.* English: "but," "although"

Examples:

haru no no ni	Planning to gather
wakana tsuman to	The tender young greens, I came
koshi *mono o*	To the springtime fields,

> chirikau hana ni   *But* showers of scattering petals
> michi wa madoinu   Made me wander from the path.
> (KKS 116)

Roku o tamawaramu to omoitsuru *mono o*, tamawarazu narinuru koto: I thought I would receive a reward, *but* it is certain now that I won't! (*Mak.*)

Note: *Mono no* has essentially the same meaning.

Example:

Tanomanu *mono no*, koitsutsu furu: *Although* I don't trust you, I go on loving you. (*Ise*)

b. As an exclamatory phrase

As indicated above, *mono o* in final position usually suggests unhappiness on the part of the speaker. MJ: *de aru no ni nā*; English: "but alas!" Occasionally, however, it functions as a simple exclamation (example 3 below).

Examples:

Ge ni yukashikaritsuru *mono o*: I was really curious [to see what would happen], but now . . . (*Mak.*)

Yo wa midaretarishikadomo miyako ni wa kaku nakarishi *mono o*: Though the world was in turmoil, it was never like this [while we were] in the capital. (*Heike*)

Imada ikite sōrau to kikoshimesaresōrawaba, sadamete senjin wa shitsuran *mono o* to oboshimesaresōrae: If Your Excellency hears that I am still alive, please think, "*Aha!* He must *certainly* have been the first rider [to cross the river]!" (*Heike*)

Mono Yue, *see* **Mono Kara**

Mono Zo

Mono zo is an emphatic combination of particles, corresponding to MJ *ni chigai nai.* It may appear as *mono so* in early texts.

Example:

Akikaze no tachikuru toki ni mono omou *mono so*: *Ah!* He must have sad thoughts when the autumn wind comes blowing. (MYS 2626)

Mo Zo, *see* **Mo Koso**

Na

The particle *na* may have either an exclamatory or a negative sense.

a. As an exclamatory particle, *na* occurs in final position, often preceded by *ka*. See also **Ka Na.**

Examples:

Ureshū mo mata tsumitsuru ka *na*: How happy I am! It has piled up again! (*Mak.*)

Miya no arisama yori mo, masaritamaeru ka *na*: He is even superior to the prince! (*Genji*)

b. *Na* may follow the *shūshikei* to form a negative imperative. See also *na . . . so*, p. 71.

Examples:
Shirayama no Kannon, kore kiesasetamau *na*: Shirayama Kannon, *don't let* this melt. (*Mak.*)
Kano sato yori kitaran hito ni, kaku kikasu *na*: *Don't tell* this to anyone who comes from that house. (*Mak.*)

Nado and its Variant **Nando**
Nado follows substantives, adverbs, particles, etc.
a. As in MJ, it may mean "and so forth."

Example:
Yone, io *nado* koeba, okonaitsu: Since they begged for rice, fish, *and so forth*, we gave them things. (*Tosa*)

b. In Heian literature, in particular, it occurs frequently as a device for making a statement less positive.

Examples:
Ame *nado* furu mo okashi: It is also interesting when it rains. (*Mak.*)
Mashite kari *nado* no tsuranetaru ga ito chiisaku miyuru, ito okashi: And of course it is much more interesting to see a file of wild geese looking very tiny. (*Mak.*)

c. It may indicate that a preceding quotation is inexact. In such a context, *nado te* may appear as a contraction of *nado tote*.

Example:
Hitozama mo yoki hito ni owasu, nado iitari: He said, "Besides, he's very handsome" [or words to that effect]. (*Take.*)

Nagara
The conjunctive particle *nagara* follows substantives, the *ren'yōkei* of verbs and verb-type suffixes (*jodōshi*), the *shūshikei* of shiku-type adjectives, and the stems of other adjectives and of adjective-type suffixes (*jodōshi*).
1. It may function as a conditional-conjunctive particle resembling *tsutsu* and indicating:
a. Unchanging continuation of an act or state. MJ: [*no*] *mama de*

Example:
Hana iroiro ni sakimidaretaru o miyarite, fushi *nagara* kaku zo iwaruru: We were looking out at the flowers, blooming in

a riot of different colors; and *while* we were *still* lying there, we [thought of and] recited poems [without premeditation], thus. . . . (*Kagerō nikki*)

b. Simultaneous acts. MJ: *shi tsutsu, shi nagara*

Example:
Kakaru ori ni, mukai naru ōchi no ki ni hōshi no noborite ki no mata ni tsuiite monomiru ari. [Eda ni] toritsuki *nagara* itō neburite: At that point, I noticed a monk who had climbed into a China-tree opposite us and was straddling a limb, watching the spectacle. He was holding onto [the branch] and fighting off sleep *at the same time* . . . (TZG)

2. It may function as a concessive conjunctive particle resembling *mono kara* and *mono no*. MJ: *keredomo, ga, nagara*

Examples:
Hi wa teri *nagara*, yuki no kashira ni furikakarikeru o yomasetamai-keru: *Although* the sun was shining, snow was falling on his head, and she had him compose a poem about it. (KKS 8)
Koremori no kyō wa, migara wa Yashima ni ari *nagara*, kokoro wa miyako e kayowarekeri: *Although* Lord Koremori's body was at Yashima, his heart was in the capital. (*Heike*)

Note: After a substantive or adverb, *nagara* may function as an inclusive adverbial particle. MJ: *sokkuri, tomo ni, gurumi*; English: "and all," "both," "all," "altogether," "including"

Example:
Tsubo *nagara* tōku sutemu: [Because there are snakes inside] I'll throw it far away, jar *and all*. (*Konjaku monogatari*)

Naku Ni

Naku ni is the nominalized form of the suffix *zu* (for which see **Aku**) plus the particle *ni*. It may indicate:

1. An emphatic negative statement. MJ: *nai koto yo, nai koto da nā*

Example:

oshimedomo	Much as it grieves me,
todomara*naku ni*	The season *will not linger*.
harugasumi	Complaints are useless,
kaeru michi ni shi	For already the spring haze
tachinu to omoeba	Has risen to start for home.
	(KKS 130)

2. A concessive negative statement. MJ: *nai no ni, nai ni mo kakawarazu*

48

Example:

mezurashiki	You sing, o cuckoo,
koe nara*naku ni*	With a voice familiar
hototogisu	And by no means rare—
kokora no toshi o	*Yet* listening through the years
akazu mo aru ka na	We never weary of you. (KKS 359)

Namu and its Variant Nan

The emphatic particle *namu* occurs after substantives, *rentaikei* forms, adverbs, and particles. It is usually followed by a *rentaikei* (see p. 71), but may itself sometimes occur in final position, in which case a following verb, usually *ari* or *nari*, is implied.

Examples:

Ito katakute, ōku *nan* aritsuru: [The snow] was very hard, and there was [*indeed*] a great deal of it. (*Mak.*)

Kyō made wa amarikoto ni *nan*: For it to have lasted until today would have been too much! (*Mak.*)

Note: Do not confuse with the suffix-like particle *namu*, indicating hope or demand, that follows the *mizenkei*, or with the *mizenkei na* of *nu* plus *mu*.

Ni

The particle *ni* appears most frequently in literary Japanese as a dative, instrumental, or locative case particle (in, on, at, to, by, for), and as a conjunctive particle. Do not confuse it with the *ren'yōkei ni* of the *shitei* 指定 (*dantei* 断定) suffix *nari*, for which see the note under **Nite.**.

1. The case-particle uses resemble those of MJ.

Examples:

Mono *ni* irete: We put it *in* something . . . (*Mak.*)

Kono yama tsukuru hito *ni* wa, hi mikka tabubeshi: We intend to give three days [of vacation] *to* people who [help] build this mountain. (*Mak.*)

Tsugomorigata *ni*: *Toward* the last day of the year. (*Mak.*)

2. The conjunctive-particle *ni* follows the *rentaikei*. It has four principal uses.

a. It may indicate that the preceding sequence is a temporal condition for the following sequence. The following sequence frequently ends with a copula, indicating what one has discovered or become aware of as a result of the preceding sequence. MJ: *to*, *-tara*. English: "when," "upon"

Examples:

Ayashigarite yorite miru *ni*, tsutsu no naka hikaritari: He wondered about it, and *when* he drew near and looked, he found that a light was shining inside the stalk. (*Take*.)

Hi no naka ni uchikubete yakasetamau *ni*, meramera to yakenu: *When* he had them put [the fur robe] in the fire, it burned fiercely. (*Take*.)

b. It may indicate that the preceding sequence is a cause of, or reason for, the following sequence. MJ: *no de, kara*. English: "because," "since"

Examples:
> Kishimeku *ni*, odorokasetamaite: *Because* it squeaked, Her Majesty woke up. (*Mak*.)
>
> Kamishimo o erabazu waka o shō sesasetamawan *ni*, ge ni iramahoshiki koto ni haberedo: *Since* His Majesty intended to judge the poems without reference to [the authors'] statuses, it was certainly an event people wanted to participate in, but . . . (*Ōkagami*)

c. It may connect two sequences that are in contrast. The contrast is often between an expectation expressed or implied in the preceding sequence and the actual result or situation described in the following sequence. MJ: *no ni, keredomo*. English: "although," "but"

Example:
> Nioi nado wa kari no mono naru *ni* . . . enaranu nioi ni wa kanarazu kokorodokimeki suru mono nari: *Although* scent is only a temporary thing, how fast our hearts always beat when we smell some marvelous fragrance! (TZG)

d. It may indicate that the following sequence is in addition to the preceding sequence. MJ: *sono ue sara ni*. English: "in addition to," "and furthermore"

Example:
> Monofuritaru mori no keshiki mo tada naranu ni tamagaki o shi watashite sakaki ni yū kaketaru nado imijikaranu ka wa: The ancient forests have a special atmosphere, *and* the surrounding shrine fences and the *sakaki* trees with their sacred cloth strips are *also* most impressive. (TZG)

3. Other uses
   a. After a substantive, *ni* may indicate character or manner of being. It occurs frequently in such sequences as *A o B ni omou*, "to regard A as B," "to think of A as being B."
   MJ: *to, to shite*. English: "as," "as being"

50

Example:
> Koromo o katami *ni* mitamae: Please look on the robe *as* a keepsake. (*Take.*)

b. It may indicate cause.

Example:
> Fukimayou kaze *ni*, tokaku utsuriyuku: [The fire] spread here and there *because* of the wind that was blowing from every direction. (*Hōjōki*)

c. When *ni* stands between a *ren'yōkei* and another form of the same verb, it acts as an intensifying particle.

Example:
> Za ni tada tsuki *ni* tsukitarishi, asamashiku haberishi koto zo ka shi: It was most shocking indeed that he simply sat *right down* on a seat. (*Ōkagami*)

Ni Shite

The phrase *ni shite* has three common uses.
1. It may indicate place. MJ: *ni atte, ni oite, de*

Examples:
> Tsuchi *ni shite* wa, Susanoo no mikoto yori zo okorikeru: *On* earth, it began with Sasanoo no mikoto. (*KKS* preface)
> Senjō *ni shite* utaruru daishu sen'yonin: The monks slain on the field of battle numbered more than 1,000. (*Heike*)

2. It may indicate age.

Example:
> Misoji amari *ni shite* . . . hitotsu no iori o musubu: *In my* thirties I built a simple house. (*Hōjōki*)

3. It may be identical in meaning with the copular *ni/nite*. MJ: *de atte*

Example:
> Geshō no mi *ni shite*: *Being* someone of inferior birth. (*Konjaku monogatari*)

Nite

The particle *nite*, classified as a case particle (*kakujoshi* 格助詞), follows substantives or the equivalent. It has the following uses.
a. It may indicate location in space or time. MJ: *ni, de*

Examples:
> Shinobine no goro *nite*: *At* the time for quiet song. (*Ōkagami*)

Hito no kuni *nite* mo, kakaru koto wa taezu zo arikeru: Even *in* other provinces, that sort of thing happened constantly. (*Ise*)

b. It may indicate instrument or means. MJ: *de*; English: "with," "by means of"

Example:
Gojūyoki *nite* fusegitatakaikeredomo: Although they defended it *with* over fifty horsemen . . . (*Heiji monogatari*)

c. It may indicate cause, reason, proof, or motive. MJ: *no tame, ni yotte, de*

Example:
Take no naka ni owasuru *nite* shirinu. Ko to naritamubeki hito nameri: I know it *because* she was inside the bamboo. She must be meant to be our child. (*Take*.)

Note: The case particle *nite* should not be confused with:
1. The form produced by the *ren'yōkei ni* of the suffix *nu* plus the conjunctive particle *te*.
2. The copular combination formed by the copular *ni* and the conjunctive particle *te*.

The copular particle *de* almost never appears before the Kamakura period. Instead, early *bungo* uses *ni* or *nite*. This *ni* occurs with *ari* as *ni ari*, which is an alternative form of the *shitei* 指定 suffix *nari*; and which, like *nari*. performs the same function as MJ *de aru* or *desu*. When this *ni* stands alone or with *te* in medial position, it acts as the *ren'yōkei* of *nari*. It has two closely related uses.

a. It may indicate a situation or condition. MJ: *to shite*

Examples:
Ichi no miko wa, udaijin no nyōgo no on-hara *nite*, yose omoku: *As* the offspring of the Minister of the Right's daughter, the First Prince enjoyed powerful support. (*Genji*)
Mukashi, otoko, Ise no saigū ni, uchi no on-tsukai *nite* mairerikereba: Once when a man visited the Ise Virgin *as* a messenger from the Emperor . . . (*Ise*)

b. It may serve as a connective between two sequences or between a statement and *ari*. MJ: *de*

Examples:
Takaki tokoro *nite*, koko kashiko sōbōdomo arawa ni miorosaru: It *was* a high place, *and so* one could look down and plainly see the monks' dwellings here and there. (*Genji*)
Makoto ni go-fubin nari to no go-kishoku *nite* sōrawaba: If your feeling *is* truly one of compassion. (*Heiji monogatari*)

> Jōkō toriaesasetamawanu on-arisama *nite* mi-kuruma ni mesarekeri:
> Looking flustered, the Retired Emperor got into the carriage.
>
> (*Heiji monogatari*)
>
> Note: As in the second example, *sōrau* or another substitute may replace *ari*.

No (*See also* Ga)

The primary use of *no* is as a case particle.

1. Attributive case

No may indicate an attributive relationship between a preceding word or phrase and a following substantive. MJ: *no*. The following are typical contexts.

a. Between two substantives

(1) Possession, affiliation, attachment, etc.

> Example:
> Fushōdono *no* o-uma nite sōrau: It is Lord Fushō'*s* horse. (TZG)
> Ume *no* hana o mite yomeru: Composed when he saw the blossoms *of* the plum. (KKS)

(2) Apposition

> Example:
> Shi-no-kimi no on-hara *no* [= de aru] himegimi: The daughter, Shi-no-kimi's child. (*Genji*)

b. Between an adjective stem or uninflected adjective and a substantive

> Example:
> Ana, medeta *no* Giō gozen no saiwai ya: Ah, what splendid fortune Lady Giō enjoys! (*Heike*)

c. Between an adverb and a substantive

> Example:
> Tokaku *no* koto naku . . . suguru hito ari: There are those who will go along . . . without [saying] anything one way or the other. (TZG)

d. Between a quasi-substantive (e.g. *kimi ya komu ware ya yukamu* in the example below) and a substantive

> Example:
>
> | | |
> |---|---|
> | kimi ya komu | While I asked myself |
> | ware ya yukamu *no* | Whether you might be coming |
> | isayoi ni | Or I might go there, |
> | maki no itado mo | The hesitant moon appeared, |
> | sasazu nenikeri | And I slept, the door unlocked. |
>
> (KKS 690)

e. Between a rentaikei and a substantive (post-Heian)

Example:
> Moshi, isasaka mo ko taru *no* michi o shiraba: If he had any understanding whatever of filial duty. (Bakin)

Note: The MJ substantival *no*, which is possibly derived from *mono*, does not ordinarily occur in *bungo*. However, the attributive case particle *no* may function as a quasi-substantive when a following substantive is implied by the context.

Example:
> Makoto ni, kabakari *no* [ōgi no hone] wa miezaritsu: Indeed, [a fan frame] of such excellence has never been seen. (*Mak.*)

2. Nominative case

Between a substantive and a predicate, *no* functions as a nominative case marker.

a. It may indicate the subject of a subordinate clause.

Example:

uguisu *no*	If there were no songs
tani yori izuru	Of warblers venturing forth
koe naku wa	Out of the valleys,
haru kuru koto o	Who of us would be aware
tare ka shiramashi	Of the coming of springtime?
	(KKS 14)

b. It may indicate the subject in a sentence with an implied final substantive or other unusual ending.

Example:

chiru to mite	Would that I had watched
arubeki mono o	And let them scatter at will—
ume no hana	Now, alas, the scent
utate nioi *no*	From the blossoms of the plum
sode ni tomareru [koto yo]	Lingers on my sleeve. (KKS 47)

Note: *No* occasionally occurs after the subject of the main predicate in Heian texts. Instances decline later. A few cases are known from the Tokugawa period, all of which resemble *no* plus the *rentaikei* in being emphatic or exclamatory.

Example:
> Ate naru onna *no*, ama ni narite, yo no naka o omoiunjite, kyō ni arazu, haruka naru yamazato ni sumikeri: A high-born lady became a nun, conceived of society as distasteful, and lived in a remote mountain dwelling instead of staying in the capital. (*Ise*)

3. Accusative case

No occurs occasionally in *Genji monogatari* and other texts as an accusative case particle. MJ: *o*

Example:
> Asagarei *no* keshiki bakari furesasetamaite: He barely touched his meals in the Asagarei Room . . . (*Genji*)

4. Comparison

No may occur in a context where a following *gotoku* or *yō ni* is implied. In such cases, the preceding substantive is often *rei* 例. *No* also indicates a comparison (MJ: *to*) when it is followed by words like *onaji, hitoshi,* and *hitotsu.*

Examples:
> Rei *no* [gotoku] haratachi enzuru ni: As usual, she grew angry and jealous, so . . . (*Genji*)
> Waga miyo *no* onajikoto nite owashimaitsuru: He had continued to manage affairs of state just as he had done during his time on the throne. (*Genji*)

Note: Some scholars list a "complementary case" (*hokaku* 補格) to account for the use of *no* as a "complementary word" before *gotoshi, yō nari, manimani, muta,* and similar expressions. For an example with *gotoshi,* see p. 24.

O (*See also* **Mono O**)

O has three principal *bungo* uses.

1. As an accusative case particle

As a case particle, *o* is identical with MJ *o*.

a. It may indicate what in English would be called a direct object.

Examples:
> Okina take *o* toru koto hisashiku narinu: The old man's bamboo-cutting went on for a long time. (*Take.*)
> Kono ko *o* mitsukete nochi ni: After finding this child . . . (*Take.*)

b. It may occur in a related use, still found in MJ, for which there is no English counterpart.

Examples:
> Michi *o* yuku: Go along a road.
> Ie *o* sumu: Live in a house.
> Fune *o* agaru: Get out of a boat.

2. As a conjunctive particle (usually follows the *rentaikei*). This use, which does not occur in MJ, is frequently encountered in *bungo.*

a. It may indicate the existence of a definite relationship, either causative or concessive, between the preceding sequence and the following sequence.

(1) As a causal conjunctive particle (MJ: *no de, da kara*), it can usually be translated "since," "because."

> Examples:
>> Hito nakute ashikameru *o*, sarubeki hitobito, yūzukete koso wa mukaesasetamawame: *Since* it will be inconvenient for you without attendents, you had better send for some suitable women this evening. (*Genji*)
>> Shishikorashitsuru toki wa, utate haberu *o*, toku koso kokoromisasetamawame: It would be awkward to make a mistake, *so* you had better try him at once. (*Genji*)

(2) As a concessive conjunctive particle (MJ: *no ni, keredomo*), it can usually be translated "but," "although."

> Examples:
>> Hiru wa sate mo magirawashitamau *o*, yūgure to nareba, imijiku kushitamaeba: She managed to find distractions during the daytime, *but* she grew very depressed when evening came, and so . . . (*Genji*)

b. It may simply form a weak link between two independent statements, between a statement and a question, etc. In such cases, it corresponds to *ga* in MJ sentences such as the following:
> Watakushi wa Nishida desu *ga* Hori-san wa oide ni narimasu ka: My name is Nishida; is Mr. Hori in?

> Examples:

natsu no yo wa	Now that dawn has come
mada yoi nagara	Before the end of evening
akenuru *o*	On this summer night,
kumo no izuku ni	In what cloudy hostelry
tsuki yadoruran	Might the moon have gone to rest?
	(KKS 166)

> Mono-osoroshiki yo no sama nameru *o*, tonobito nite haberamu: It is a frightful night; I will act as your watchman. (*Genji*)

Note: Because the conjunctive uses of *o* tend to overlap, it will sometimes be necessary to select the appropriate meaning on the basis of context. Thus:
> Kaku mosu *o* minahito ina to mōsu:
> *Since* he spoke thus, everyone said, "No."
> *Although* he spoke thus, everyone said, "No."
> He spoke thus, *and* everyone said, "No."

3. The third principal use of *o* is as an interjectional or emphatic particle

(follows a variety of words and forms.) This is the commonest use in pre-Heian texts. The case-particle use, which is apparently a later development, is seldom found before 800.

a. In medial position

Example:
Hototogisu koko ni chikaku *o* kinakite yo: Come and sing, *oh!* close to here, cuckoo. (MYS)

b. In final position
A final exclamatory *o* usually follows a substantive, *meireikei*, or *shūshikei*. It often implies regret on the part of the speaker (cf *mono o*). MJ: *na no ni*; English: "but alas!"

Examples:
Sono yaegaki *o*: O! That manifold fence! (*Kojiki*)

tsui ni yuku	Upon this pathway,
michi to wa kanete	I have long heard others say,
kikishikado	Man sets forth at last—
kinō kyō to wa	Yet I had not thought to go
omowazarishi *o*	So very soon as today! (KKS 861)

tsuyu o nado	Why did I label
ada naru mono to	Dewdrops as evanescent?
omoiken	My life was not spent
waga mi mo kusa ni	Clinging to a blade of grass:
okanu bakari *o*	That is the only difference!
	(KKS 860)

O Ba

The phrase *o ba* combines the case particle *o* and the voiced form of the adverbial particle *wa*. It emphasizes what precedes it, often with the implied meaning "especially" or "whatever may be the case with X, Y at least."

Examples:
Na *o ba* Sakaki no Miyakko to namu iikeru: As for his name, *that* was Sakaki no Miyakko. (*Take*.)
Sono goro Kamakuradono ni Ikezuki, Surusumi to iu meiba ari. Ikezuki *o ba* Genda Kagesue shikiri ni nozomi-mōshikeredomo: Around that time, the Lord of Kamakura had [two] excellent horses called Ikezuki and Surusumi. [I don't know who might have been asking for Surusumi, but] Kajiwara Genda Kagesue kept asking for *Ikezuki*. However . . .
(*Heike*)

Raku, *see* **Aku**
Rayu, *see* **Mizenkei,** *ru/raru,* p. 9
Sae, *see* **Dani**
Seba, *see* p. 14

Shi

Shi is an emphatic medial particle. It often appears in conditional clauses.

Examples:

Wasuraruru toki *shi* nakereba: Because there is *never* a time when I can forget . . . (KKS)

Seki *shi* masashiki mono naraba: If the barrier is *indeed* a true [reliable] thing . . . (KKS)

Fune o *shi* zo omou: All my thoughts are with the boat. (KKS)

Shi Mo

Shi mo is a combination of particles that adds emphasis to what precedes it. It occurs in medial position.

Example:

yo ya kuraki	Might you find the night
michi ya madoeru	Too dark, or have you then lost
hototogisu	Your way, o cuckoo
waga yado o *shi mo*	Pouring forth your song as though
sugigate ni naku	Unable to pass my house [*in particular*]? (KKS 154)

Shite

Shite may appear as a case, conjunctive, or adverbial particle.

1. Case particle use

After a substantive or the equivalent, *shite* forms an adverbial phrase. It may be used in any of the following ways.

a. To indicate the means or method by which an act is performed. MJ: *de, o tsukatte, o motte*

Example:

Mizu o mo te *shite* sasagete nomikeru o mite: Seeing that he drank by *using* his hands to scoop up the water. (TZG)

b. To indicate a surrogate actor, the recipient-executor of a command, etc. MJ: *ni, ni meijite*

Example:

Katawara naru hito *shite* iwasureba: I *had* a nearby lady recite a poem, whereupon . . . (*Mak.*)

c. To designate persons participating in an action, and to indicate their number, which may or may not include the principal actor. MJ: *de*

Examples:

Moto yori tomo to suru hito hitori futari *shite* ikikeri: He went with one or two old friends. (*Ise*)

Kurō hitori *shite* ika de ka yo o shizumubeki: How could Kurō pacify the country by himself? (*Genpei seisuiki*)

Nishi no mon o ba, Rokujō no Hangan Tameyoshi uketamawarite, fushi rokunin *shite* katametari: Rokujō no Hangan Tameyoshi received responsibility for the west gate, and he guarded it with six men—[himself] the father and his [five] sons. (*Hōgen monogatari*)

Note: *Shite* occasionally appears in other contexts—e.g. in phrases like *sore yori shite*. Its function in such cases is said to be to improve the rhythm of the sentence.

2. Conjunctive particle use

When *shite* functions as a conjunctive particle, it can be regarded as generally equivalent in meaning to *te*. It may appear:

a. In the phrase *ni shite*. See **Ni Shite**

b. At the end of an adverbial phrase (follows *ren'yōkei*). MJ: *-te, sono yō na jōtai de*

Examples:

Chikara o irezu *shite*, tenchi o ugokashi: It moves heaven and earth without effort. (KKS preface)

Haru wa fujinami o miru. Shiun no gotoku *shite*, saihō ni niou: In the spring I see waves of wisteria. They glow in the west like purple clouds. (*Hōjōki*)

c. Linking two words or phrases, both of which have the same syntactic relationship to other elements in the sentence.

Example:

Tada kari no iori nomi, nodokeku *shite* osore nashi: It is only a temporary hut that is peaceful and safe. (*Hōjōki*)

3. Adverbial particle use

As an adverbial particle, *shite* adds emphasis.

Example:

Nani ōsu. Ima, kane sukoshi ni koso anare. Ureshiku *shite* [MJ: ureshiku mo mā] okosetaru ka na: "What is he saying? I'll have almost no money left. But how happy I am that he has sent [the robe]!" (*Take.*)

So, see **Zo.** The usual pronounciation in the Nara period was *so*. For *na . . . so*, see p. 71.

Sude Ni

The adverbial phrase *sude ni* has the following principal meanings.

1. Entirely, all. MJ: *sukkari, mattaku*

Example:

ame no shita	Awe overcomes me
sude ni ōite	When I see the radiance
furu yuki no	Of white flakes of snow
hikari o mireba	Fluttering down to cover
tōtōku mo aru ka	*Everything* under heaven.

(MYS 3923)

2. Already; for some time now. Precedes a statement indicating completion, past tense, etc. MJ: *mō, izen kara*

Example:
> Kimi ni yori wa ga na wa *sude ni* tatsu: Because of you, my name has *already* become a subject of gossip. (MYS 3931)

3. Soon, presently. Usually accompanies a conjecture. MJ: *mō sukoshi de, ma mo naku*

Examples:
> *Sude ni* fune idasubeshi tote hishimekiaeba: When they began to shout, thinking that they would *soon* be sending the ship off . . .
> (*Heike*)
> Kyūchū *sude ni* ayauku miekeru o: Although the shrine seemed to be in *imminent* danger . . . (*Heike*)

4. Actually, undeniably, precisely, just. MJ: *chōdo, hotondo, gen ni, masa ni, masashiku, tashika ni*

Example:
> Kono shōshō wa, *sude ni* kano dainagon ga chakushi nari: This Captain is *none other than* the legitimate heir of that Major Counselor. (*Heike*)

Note: *Sude ni shite* is a conjunctival phrase meaning "soon," "in due course," "meanwhile." MJ: *yagate, saru hodo ni, sōkō shite iru uchi ni*

Example:
> *Sude ni shite* kuraku narikeri: Meanwhile it grew dark.

Sura, *see* **Dani**

Te

The conjunctive particle *te* is a development from the *ren'yōkei* of the suffix *tsu*. (Since the *ren'yōkei* of *tsu* tends to appear in combination with *ki* and *keri* in such forms as *teki, teshi,* and *tekeri,* it will usually be possible to distinguish between the two without difficulty.) It follows particles (*to, ni*) and the *ren'yōkei*. When it follows a *ren'yōkei* modified by sound change (*onbin*), it may become *de*. Its principal uses are listed below.

1. When *te* links two clauses, it may act as a subordinating conjunction, indicating cause, reason, or situation; or it may act as a concessive conjunctive particle.

   a. Indication of cause or reason. MJ: *no de, tame ni*

   > Example:
   > Sawaru koto ari*te*, nao onaji tokoro nari: *Since* there is a hindrance [to our departure], we are still in the same place. (*Tosa*)

   b. Indication of situation (preceding clause becomes adverbial).

   > Example:
   > Sore o mireba, sanzun bakari naru hito, ito utsukushū*te* itari: When he looked at it, there was somebody about three inches tall, sitting very *cutely*. (*Take.*)

   c. Indication of concession. MJ: *no ni, -te wa iru ga*

   > Example:
   > Mukashi otoko, mi wa iyashiku*te*, ito takaki hito o omoikaketarikeri: Once there was a man who, *although* his position was humble, had fallen in love with someone of very high rank. (*Ise*)

2. *Te* may link two or more clauses, which together form a temporal sequence. English: "and," participial construction. MJ: *-te, soshite*

   > Example:
   > Aru hito agata no yotose itsutose hate*te*, rei no kotodomo mina shioe*te*, geyu nado tori*te*, sumu tachi yori ide*te*, fune ni norubeki tokoro e wataru: A certain man, his four- or five-year term of provincial duty having ended, completed all his prescribed tasks, received his certificate of clearance, left the official residence where he had been living, and went to the place where he was to board ship. (*Tosa*)

3. *Te* may serve as a coordinating particle between two or more words that have the same syntactic relationship to other elements in the sentence.

   > Examples:
   > Fukuraka ni*te* utsukushū owasureba: Since he was plump and appealing . . . (*Eiga monogatari*)
   > Kabeshiro wa shiroku*te* atarashi: The curtains were white and new. (*Utsubo monogatari*)

To

In general, *to* functions as in MJ. The following points may be noted. (*See also* **Tomo**)

a. *To* as a quotative particle

When *to* indicates a quotation, it follows the *shūshikei*. The verb modified by the *to* clause (e.g. *iu, omou, kiku*) may be omitted. When this *to* is followed by *no* and a substantive, the quotation modifies the substantive.

Examples:

Hayaku usehaberinikeri *to* iu: "It has already disappeared completely," she said. (*Mak.*)

Izukata ni motomeyukamu *to* kado ni idete: He went outside the gate, [wondering] where to search. (*Ise*)

Makoto ni go-fubin nari *to* no go-kishoku nite sōrawaba: If your feeling is truly one of compassion . . . (*Heiji monogatari*)

b. *To* as an expression of function, role, condition, parity, similarity, etc. MJ: *to shite*. English: "as," "for," "in the capacity of," "like," "than"

Examples:

Momijiba wa ame *to* furu tomo: Though maple leaves rain down [fall *like* rain] . . . (KKS)

Fune ni notte wa kajitori no mōsu koto o koso takaki yama *to* tanome: When I ride in a boat, I trust in the steersman's words *as* in a high mountain. (*Take.*)

c. *To* as an intensifier

When *to* occurs between the *ren'yōkei* and another form of the same verb, it intensifies the verb's meaning. It may be followed by *shi, mo,* or another particle.

Iki *to* shi ikeru mono: All living things [without exception].
(KKS preface)

Tomo and its Variant **To**

The concessive conjunctive particle *tomo* and its rarer variant *to* usually follow the *shūshikei* of verbs (also *rentaikei* from around the twelfth century on) and the *ren'yōkei* (or *mizenkei*, according to one theory) of adjectives and of *zu*. Whereas *domo/do* ordinarily follows a statement of fact and functions as the concessive counterpart of the *izenkei* plus *ba*, *tomo/to* usually follows a hypothetical statement, or a statement of fact couched in hypothetical terms, and thus functions as the concessive counterpart of the *mizenkei* plus *ba*. MJ: *-te, -te mo*. English: "even if," "although. . . may"

a. *Tomo/to* after a hypothesis

Examples:

Yorozu ni imijiku *tomo: Although* he *may* be outstanding in all respects . . . (TZG)

62

Aitatakawamu to su *tomo* kano kuni no hito kinaba takeki kokoro tsukau hito yomo araji: *Although* you *may* try to fight, I am sure there will be nobody with a brave heart if the people from that country come. (*Take.*)

b. *Tomo/to* after a statement of fact

Tomo/to, by couching a statement of fact in hypothetical terms, conveys an emphasis that would be lacking if *domo/do* were used.

Example:

Kakushite komete ari *tomo* kano kuni no hito koba mina akinamu to su: *Even though* you *may be* shutting me up in this way, all [the doors] will certainly fly open if the people from that country come. (*Take.*)

Tote

Tote is a combination of the case particle *to* and the conjunctive particle *te*. It has the following principal uses.

1. It indicates that the preceding substantive is the name of something. MJ: *to itte*

Example:

Kaikotsukoku *tote* ebisu no kowaki kuni ari: There was a powerful barbarian state *called* Kaikotsukoku. (TZG)

2. After an inflected adjective, verb, suffix, quotation, etc., it may indicate:

a. That the act or condition described in the preceding clause is a reason or cause for what follows. MJ: *to itte, kara to itte*

Examples:

Ichigyō Ajari wa daibon no hito nareba *tote*, Anketsudō e zo tsukawashikeru: Considering Ichigyō Ajari to be a major criminal, they [*therefore*] sent him to the Anketsudō Road. (*Heike*)

Gonin no naka ni, yukashiki mono o misetamaeramu ni, onkokorozashi masaritari *tote* tsukōmatsuramu: When one of the five shows me something I want, I will consider it evidence that his love for me exceeds that of the others, *and so* I will be his. (*Take.*)

b. That the act or situation described in the preceding clause represents the purpose or objective of what follows. MJ: *to omotte*

Example:

Yumi tsuyō hikamu *tote*, kore mo kabuto wa kizarikeri: *In order to be able to* draw his bow strongly, he, too, had left off his helmet. (*Heike*)

c. A quotation
> Kore mairasetamae *tote*, on-suzuri nado sashiiru: Saying, "Please present these," he thrust the inkstone and so forth inside [the blinds]. (*Mak.*)

Tsutsu

The conjunctive particle *tsutsu* follows the *ren'yōkei*. It has the following principal uses.

1. It may indicate repetition of an act. MJ: *-te wa*

Example:
> Noyama ni majirite, take o tori*tsutsu*, yorozu no koto ni tsukaikeri: Making his way into the fields and mountains, he would [*repeatedly*] gather bamboo, which he put to all manner of uses. (*Take.*)

a. When the affected verb has a plural subject, the repetition may derive from single acts performed by two or more persons.

Example:

hitogoto ni	People all play with them,
orikazashi*tsutsu*	Break*ing* them off
asobedomo	To decorate their hair—
iya mezurashiki	Yet these blossoms of the plum
ume no hana ka mo	Seem more and more precious.
	(MYS 828)

2. It may indicate simultaneous performance of two acts. MJ: *nagara*

Example:

hana mi*tsutsu*	Waiting for someone
hito matsu toki wa	*While* gazing at the flowers,
shirotae no	All unconsciously
sode ka to nomi zo	I find myself wondering:
ayamaterekeru	Might those be his pure white sleeves? (KKS 274)

3. It may indicate progress or continuation of an act.

Example:

amazakaru	For five years I *have been living*
hina ni itsutose	In a country place
sumai*tsutsu*	Remote as the heavens,
miyako no teburi	And thus I have forgotten
wasuraenikeri	The ways of the capital. (MYS 880)

4. It may sometimes be translatable as a concessive. MJ: *no ni, ni mo kaka-warazu*

Example:

wa ga kokoda	*Though* you listen alone,
matedo kinakanu	You don't tell me
hototogisu	About the cuckoo
hitori kiki*tsutsu*	That doesn't come here to sing
tsugenu kimi ka mo	No matter how much I wait.
	(MYS 4208)

5. At the end of a sentence, it combines an exclamatory function with the idea of progress, repetition, or continuation.

Example:

yamazato wa	Of the year's seasons,
aki koso koto ni	Autumn is the loneliest
wabishikere	At a mountain house.
shika no naku ne ni	Awakened by the stag's call,
me o samashi*tsutsu*	How often I lie *sleepless*!
	(KKS 214)

6. Its meaning may be identical with that of the simple conjunctive *te*, which it may replace in order to improve the rhythm of a sentence.

Example:

Yagate mairamu tote, niwaka ni shōjin hajime*tsutsu*, Itsukushima e zo mairarekeru: Saying, "I will go at once," he immediately began the purification rituals, *and then* he went to Itsukushima. (*Heike*)

Uchi

The verbal prefix *uchi* often seems to have little or no semantic function. The following points may, however, be noted.

1. As a prefix to a verb of quiet action, *uchi* may convey the sense of MJ *chotto* or *sukoshi*. English: "just a little"

Example:

Toki no ma no keburi to mo narinan to zo *uchi*miru yori omowaruru: The moment one *glances* at it, one instinctively thinks, "It will undoubtedly become transient smoke." (TZG)

2. As a prefix to a verb of vigorous action, *uchi* may intensify the act.

Example:

*Uchi*waraite: He *roared with* laughter. (*Genji*)

Wa

Wa is primarily a separative or distinguishing particle that marks out a preceding word, clarifies its syntactic function, and/or establishes a special relationship between it and the main predicate of the clause or sentence. Some important uses are listed below.

1. Distinguishing particle in medial position. Follows substantives or the equivalent, inflected words, particles, etc. (Note that although it often follows the subject of a clause or sentence, it is not a nominative case particle, since it also occurs after direct and indirect objects. When it follows the accusative case particle *o*, it changes to *ba*. *See* **O Ba**) It may indicate:

   a. Special comment or emphasis

Examples:

saku hana wa	Flowers that bloom [ostentatiously]
utsurou toki ari	Will scatter in their season.
ashihiki no	What *truly* endures
yamasuga no ne shi	Is the [unpretentious] root
nagaku *wa* arikeri	Of the mountain sedge. (MYS 4484)

Hajime yori ware *wa* to omoiagaritamaeru on-katagata: Ladies who had thought confidently from the outset, "*I* [am certain to become the favorite]." (*Genji*)

   b. A contrastive relationship

Example:

koe *wa* shite	You raise your sad *voice*,
namida *wa* mienu	O cuckoo, in plaintive cries,
hototogisu	Yet I cannot see
waga koromode no	That you have shed any *tears*.
hitsu o karanamu	Won't you borrow my drenched sleeves? (KKS 149)

   c. A topic

Example:

Ariwara no Narihira *wa*, kokoro amarite kotoba tarazu: *As for* Ariwara no Narihira, the emotion [in his poems] is excessive and the words are too few. (KKS preface)

   d. Existence of a situation
      (1) Actual

Example:

Tadaima no gotoku nite *wa*, yukusue sae kokorobosoki ni: With the situation as it was now, the future, too, must be uncertain . . . (*Kagerō nikki*)

      (2) Hypothetical

Example:

omou hodo	Of what use is love
shirade *wa* kai ya	*If* we cannot gauge its depth?

arazaramu	I would like to see
kaesugaesu mo	The boundless devotion
kazu o koso mime	Of which you tell me.

(*Kagerō nikki*)

2. Subjective particle

When *wa* occurs after the *ren'yōkei* of an inflected adjective, or an adjective-type suffix (*jodōshi*), or of the negative suffix *zu*, it indicates conjecture about a situation contrary to fact. MJ: *moshi, nara*. From late Heian on, *zu wa* often becomes *zu ba*, which has an emphatic variant, *zunba*.

Example:

uguisu no	If there were no songs
tani yori izuru	Of warblers venturing forth
koe naku *wa*	Out of the valleys,
haru kuru koto o	Who of us would be aware
tare ka shiramashi	Of the coming of springtime?

(KKS 14)

3. Final particle

In final position, *wa* follows a substantive or a *rentaikei*, or combines with another particle in such expressions as *ya wa, ka wa,* and *zo wa*. It conveys emotion or emphasis.

Examples:

Sari tomo, tsui ni otoko awasezaran ya *wa*: Even so, is it likely that they won't arrange a match for her eventually? [Of course not!]
(*Take.*)

kyō yori wa	Today I set out,
kaerimi nakute	Never to look back:
ōkimi no	*Yes, I,* who go forth
shiko no mitate to	To serve as our great lord's
idetatsu ware *wa*	Impregnable shield! (MYS 4373)

Wo, *see* **O**

Ya

Like *ka*, *ya* functions both as an interrogative and as an interjectional particle. (As in MJ, it may also link two substantives. Since that use presents no problems, it is not discussed here.) The two uses occur in comparable contexts: (1) medially, after almost any part of speech, and (2) finally, after a substantive or a *shūshikei*.

a. The interrogative *ya*

The interrogative *ya* was originally distinguished from *ka* by the fact that it was a true interrogative (a question addressed to another or to oneself), whereas *ka* expressed doubt; and also by the fact that in the Heian period *ya* always preceded question words, whereas *ka* always followed such words. *Ya* steadily encroached on *ka*, however, and it occurs in the *ka* sense in Heian texts. In the Kamakura period, *ya* begins to appear after question words.

The fact that *ya* is functioning as an interrogative is often indicated by the occurrence of *mu* or a negative in the clause or sentence.
(1) In medial position

When the interrogative *ya* occurs medially, it indicates doubt, a question, or a rhetorical question, It usually follows the *shūshikei*, but may follow the *ren'yōkei*. The final inflected form should be a *rentaikei* (*see* Kakarimusubi and Other Grammatical Patterns).

Examples:
> Kimi *ya* koshi: Might you have come? (KKS)
> Imoarai e *ya* mawarubeki: Ought we to go around toward Imoarai? (*Heike*)
> Tsuki *ya* aranu haru *ya* mukashi no haru naranu: Is not the moon the same? The spring the spring of old? (KKS)

(2) In final position

The interrogative *ya* in final position has the same three uses as in (1). It usually follows the *shūshikei*, but in poetry and in Nara-period prose it may follow the *izenkei* when a rhetorical question is intended.

Examples:
> Sate yuki wa kyō made aritsu *ya*: Well, has the snow lasted until today? (*Mak.*)
> Kome *ya* to wa omou mono kara: Although I think, "Will he come? [Of course not.]" . . . (KKS)

Note: The addition of *wa* makes the rhetorical or interrogative *ya* more emphatic.

Example:

yo no naka wa	Has life on this earth
mukashi yori *ya wa*	Given rise to human grief
ukariken	Since antiquity,
waga mi hitotsu no	Or am I the only one
tame ni nareru ka	Who finds it so hard to bear?
	(KKS 948)

b. The interjectional (exclamatory) *ya*

As an interjectional particle, *ya* indicates emotion. It often follows a word of address or a command. Especially in Nara and Heian poetry, it may precede or follow an *izenkei*. It occurs both in medial position, where it sometimes functions as an emphatic substitute for *no*, and in final position.

Examples:
> Koe taezu nake *ya* uguisu: Keep singing, warbler! Do not let your voice be still. (KKS)
>
> Shikishima *ya* koko no koto to wa miezu: It did not seem to be something happening here in Shikishima. (*Ōkagami*)
>
> Shinohara *ya* shino wakuru michi o sugiyukeba: Making his way through the bamboo of Shinohara . . . (*Taiheiki*)
>
> Sazo na wa tatsu *ya*: Ah! They will surely be talked about! (*Mak.*)
>
> Kami mo ureshi to shinobazarame *ya*: The gods, too, must be overjoyed! (*Shūishū*)

Yo

The particle *yo* has vocative and emphatic uses.

Examples:
> Tsuginobu *yo*: Tsuginobu! (*Genpei seisuiki*)
>
> Shinamu *yo* imo: I shall die [of love], girl. (MYS 581)

> Note: In the Nara period, *yo* also functioned as a case particle, indicating means, comparison, or starting point in space or time.

Yu

In texts of the Nara period, the particle *yu* has the same uses as the case particle *yo*, which see.

Example:
> Tago no ura *yu* uchiidete: Emerging *from* Tago shore. (MYS 318)

> Note: For *yu* as a suffix, see Mizenkei, *ru/raru* suffix.

Zo

Zo is an emphatic particle, similar in force to MJ *zo*. When it occurs in medial position, the final inflected form should be a *rentaikei*. (See Kakarimusubi and Other Grammatical Patterns.) In final position after a *rentaikei* or a substantive, it is equivalent to an emphatic copula (MJ: *da zo, no da zo*).

Examples:

haru kinu to	Now it is springtime,
hito wa iedomo	So everyone says—and yet
uguisu no	I cannot but feel
nakanu kagiri wa	There will be no spring until
araji to *zo* omou	The warbler sends forth his song.

(KKS 11)

> Kore, tamawasuru *zo*: This is [*nothing less than*] a present from Her Majesty. (*Mak.*)
>
> Saburaidomo o yarite torisuteshi *zo*: [*The fact is that*] I sent some attendants to get rid of it! (*Mak.*)

Zo Ka Shi

Zo ka shi is an emphatic combination of particles. It may occur in either medial or final position.

Example:
Za ni tada tsuki ni tsukitarishi, asamashiku haberishi koto *zo ka shi*: It was *most* shocking *indeed* that he simply sat right down in the seating area.
(*Ōkagami*)

Zu Ba, Zu Wa, *see* Wa

KAKARIMUSUBI AND OTHER GRAMMATICAL PATTERNS

The following are recurrent grammatical patterns with which the student should be familiar.

1. **Kakarimusubi** 係結び (bound ending)

Kakarimusubi is the Japanese term for a grammatical usage observed in the Nara and Heian periods (particularly the latter), and to a diminishing extent in the medieval (*chūsei*) period. It affects the ending of an inflected form without changing the meaning of the sentence in which the form occurs. It operates when a sentence contains the interrogative particle *ka*, the interrogative particle *ya*, the emphatic particle *namu*, the emphatic particle *zo*, or the emphatic particle *koso*. It may also be brought into play by an interrogative like *nado, tare, izuku, izure,* or *ika de* when the context permits the mental addition of *ka*. The *kakarimusubi* rule may be stated as follows:

> When *ka, namu, ya,* or *zo* occurs in medial position, the final inflected form in the same clause will be a *rentaikei*. When *koso* so occurs, the form will be an *izenkei*.

Examples:

Nosaki no tsukai tatsu nado *zo,* aware ni yangoto na*ki*: The departure of the tribute-rice messengers inspires the deepest awe. (TZG)

Furusato wa yuki to nomi *koso* hana wa chiru*rame*: At the old home, blossoms must be falling like snowflakes. (KKS 111)

Saru tokoro ni *ika de* [*ka*] mono shitama*eru* to ierikereba: Since he had said, "Why do you stay in such a place?"
(Yamato monogatari)

2. **Na . . . So** (negative imperative)

Na . . . so indicates a prohibition with overtones of a request. It seldom appears except in poetry and in quoted conversation. The usual rule is that the *ren'yōkei* of a verb appears between the *na* and the *so*; the exception to the rule is that the *mizenkei* so appears in the case of a *kahen* or *sahen* verb. A comparatively lengthy phrase or construction may sometimes separate the *na* and the *so*.

Examples:

natsuyama ni	O cuckoo singing
naku hototogisu	Amid the summer mountains:
kokoro araba	If you have feelings,
mono omou ware ni	*Do not* harrow with your voice
koe *na* kikase *so*	One whose heart already aches.

(KKS 145)

Hito *na* itaku wabisasetatẹmatsuritamai *so*: Don't make people suffer so terribly.

3. E . . . Zu (impossibility)

E, classified as an adverb, can also be thought of as a potential prefix. (Compare the *shimo nidan* verb *u*, grasp, get, use, which means "be able to" when it follows the ren'yōkei of another verb.) When it immediately precedes a verb ending in *zu* or in another negative suffix, such as *de, ji,* or *maji,* it indicates impossibility, or, occasionally, a strong negative.

Examples:

Sato tōki wa, *e* tsugeyara*zu*: We were *unable* to send word to those whose homes were distant. (*Mak.*)

Nanuka dani *e* sugusa*ji*: It probably *won't* even *be able* to last beyond the Seventh. (*Mak.*)

Nekoma-dono to wa *e* iwa*de*, Neko-dono no maremare waitaru ni mono yosoe to zo iikeru: *Without* saying, "Lord Nekoma" *at all*, he said, "Lord Cat [neko] is paying us a rare visit. Get him something to eat."

(*Heike*)

Note: The *e . . . zu* construction appears fairly often with *iu*, say, in the form *e mo iwazu* (or *e mo iwarezu*), "beyond words," "incapable of being described"; and less frequently with *naru* as *e narazu*. *E narazu* indicates a high degree of praise or approbation; *e mo iwazu*, like MJ *hijō ni*, can be either positive ("splendid") or negative ("terrible").

Examples:

Toneri sanjūnin *e mo iwazu* sōzokasete: They costumed thirty attendants *with indescribable splendor*. (*Utsubo monogatari*)

Tsuiji kado no shita nado ni mukite *e mo iwanu* kotodomo shichirashi: [Drunk men] go around doing *unspeakable* things by walls and gates.

(TZG)

On-shitsurai nado *e narazu* shite sumaikeru sama nado ge ni miyako no yangoto naki tokorodokoro ni koto narazu: [Prince Genji's] accommodations were *splendid indeed*, and the style in which [the Akashi Novice] himself lived was in no respect different from that of the most elegant mansions in the capital. (*Genji*)

LIST OF COMMON HONORIFIC, POLITE, AND HUMBLE VERBS

I

HONORIFIC (SONKEI 尊敬)

Speaker shows respect for subject of verb. MJ: *o-* . . . *ni naru*

Asobasu (tr/intr. 4): hunt, go on outing, perform music, do; may replace another V (e.g. compose, write); hon. aux. (Tokugawa and later)

Imasogari (intr. *rahen*): ari, ori

Imasu (intr. 4 in Nara and early Heian, later *sahen*): ari, ori

Imasugari (intr. *rahen*): ari, ori

Kikoshimesu (tr. 4): hear, sanction, agree to, eat, drink, perform, govern, think

Kudasaru (tr. 4 and *shimo* 2): bestow on inferior; hon. aux.

Mairu (tr. 4): eat, drink, etc.; see also humble uses

Masu (intr. 4): ari, ori, go, come; hon. aux. indicating continuation

Matsuru (tr. 4): may serve as equivalent of kikoshimesu

Mesu (tr. 4): govern, summon, capture, arrest, see, drink, eat, wear, ride, buy, do, etc.; hon. aux.

Mōsu (tr. 4): be named; see also humble and polite uses

Nasaru (tr. 4, tr. *shimo* 2): do; hon. aux.

Nasu (tr. 4): do, make, accomplish; may also appear as hon. aux. *sahen*

Oboshimesu (tr. 4): think

Ōsu (tr. *shimo* 2): say, command

Owashimasu (intr. 4): owasu plus masu; makes owasu more respectful

Owasu (intr. *sahen*; said to occur also as 4 and *shimo* 2): be, have, sit, come, go; when attached to *ren'yōkei* of V, indicates that the act and its result are both still going on, and indicates respect for actor; after *ren'yōkei* of adjective, or after a substantive plus *ni* or *to*, indicates that such-and-such a situation exists, and shows respect for subject of situation

Shiroshimesu (tr. 4): shiru (know, etc.), interfere; more exalted than shirosu

Shirosu (tr. 4): shiru (know, etc.), govern

Tabu (tr. 4): abbreviated form of tamau with same meaning; also tōbu

Tamau (tr. 4): give to an inferior; hon. aux.

Tamawaru (tr. 4): give to an inferior; hon. aux.; see also humble uses

Tamawasu (tr. *shimo* 2): give to an inferior; more honorific than tamau
Tatematsuru (tr. 4): eat, wear, ride, etc.; see also humble uses
Tōbu (tr. 4): see tabu
Watarasu (intr. *shimo* 2): wataru (cross, etc.)
Wataru (intr. 4): go, come, walk, be, be present

II

POLITE (TEINEI 丁寧)

Conveys formal attitude toward person addressed. MJ: *-masu, gozaimasu*

Haberi (intr. *rahen*): serve (an aristocrat, an emperor), be, have, sit, come; as aux., showed courtesy to the interlocutor until late Heian, when it was replaced by saburau; from Kamakura on, merely an elegant literary suffix
Hanberi: a variant of haberi
Mōsu (tr. 4): say; see also honorific and humble uses
Saburau (intr. 4): ari, ori, attend a superior, approach or visit a superior; polite aux.; see also humble uses
Samurau (intr. 4): ari, ori, come, go, live, give to a superior; used by women
Sōrau (intr. 4; a development from saburau; common in 13th and 14th centuries): attend a superior, ari, ori; from Kamakura on, polite aux.; used by men in conversation; in careless speech, contracts to *sō*. *Sa mo sōzu=sa mo sōrawanzu*
Tōbu (intr. 4): In Heian, a polite aux. attached to haberi; used mostly by men; see also honorific use

III

HUMBLE (KENJŌ 謙讓)

Shows disrespect for actor and respect for object of act. MJ: *mōshiageru*

Kikoesasu (tr. *shimo* 2): say; humble aux.

74

Kikoyu (tr. *shimo* 2): say, be called, give, send; humble aux. Do not confuse with kikoyu (intr. *shimo* 2), be audible, be intelligible, be famous, be rumored, be heard, etc.

Mairasu (tr. *shimo* 2): give to a superior; humble aux.

Mairu (tr./intr. 4): go, come, give to a superior, serve; see also honorific uses

Makaru (intr. 4): come, go, withdraw, die; as prefix, may be humble, emphatic, or solemn

Masu (tr. 4): say; see also honorific uses

Matsuru (tr. 4): give to a superior; humble aux.; see also honorific uses

Mōsu (tr. 4): say, report, ask for, govern, do (vis-a-vis a superior), invite; humble aux.; see also honorific and polite uses

Mōzu (intr. *shimo* 2): go, come, reach, go to shrine or temple

Saburau (intr. 4): ari, ori, give to a superior, come, go; see also polite uses

Sōrau (intr. 4): ari, ori; see also polite uses

Taimatsuru (tr. 4): sound change from tatematsuru, which see

Tamau (tr. *shimo* 2): eat, drink; humble aux., usually following omou, miru, or kiku (used only of speaker's act); sometimes called polite aux. Distinguish from the more common honorific tamau (4).

Tamawaru (tr. 4): receive from a superior, compose poem on topic set by a superior; see also honorific uses

Tatematsuru (tr. 4): give to a superior; humble aux.; humble suffix to an omitted V (e.g. nose-tatematsuru, kise-tatematsuru); see also honorific uses

Tsukaematsuru (tr./intr. 4): do, be in service, be a bureaucrat, be a wife; humble aux.; humble substitute for another V. Variants: tsukamatsuru, tsukōmatsuru

Uketamawaru (tr. 4): receive, hear, receive and obey an order

SOUND CHANGES (ONBIN) IN VERBS
AND ADJECTIVES

Onbin 音便 is the Japanese term for sound changes which sometimes, but not invariably, affect verbs and adjectives in certain phonetic contexts. For verbs, such changes are most frequently encountered when *ren'yōkei* forms are followed by "t." The commonest ones are listed in the outline below, which is based on Yuzawa Kōkichirō 湯沢幸吉郎, *Bungo bunpō shōsetsu* 文語文法詳説 (Yūbun Shoin 右文書院, 1959), pp. 106ff and 140ff.

I. Onbin in Verbs

There are four categories of verb *onbin*: *i-onbin, u-onbin, hatsu-onbin*, and *soku-onbin*.

A. *I-Onbin*

In this type of sound change, *i* may replace *ki, gi,* or *shi. I-onbin* may occur under the following conditions.

1. The consonant "k" or "g" may disappear when the particle *te* follows the *ren'yōkei* of a *ka*-type or *ga*-type yodan verb (e.g. naku, oyogu). If the verb is a *ga*-type, the "t" becomes "d."

   Examples:
   Nakite becomes *naite*
   Isogite becomes *isoide*

2. In texts of the Heian and later periods, *ki*, the *ren'yōkei* form of a *ka*-type *yodan* verb, sometimes becomes *i* when followed by *ta* (e.g. by a form of the suffix *tari* or of the auxiliary verb tamau), or when followed by the *so* of the negative imperative *na. . . so.*

   Examples:
   Nakitari becomes *naitari*
   Kikitamaeru becomes *kiitamaeru*
   Na naki so becomes *na nai so*

3. In texts of the Heian and later periods, *i* may replace the *ren'yōkei shi* of *sa*-type yodan verbs (e.g. obosu) if the following conditions prevail.

76

    a. If *shi* is followed by *te* or *ta*

Examples:
> *Oboshitaru* becomes *oboitaru*
> *Motenashitamau* becomes *motenaitamau*

OR b. If *shi* is followed by the suffix *shi* (*rentaikei* of *ki*)

Example:
> *Owashimashishi* becomes *owashimaishi*

4. In texts of the Kamakura and later periods, the *ren'yōkei* form *shi* of a *sa*-type yodan verb (e.g. obosu) sometimes becomes *i* before the *so* of *na. . . so.*

Example:
> *Na tomoshi so* becomes *na tomoi so*

B. *U-Onbin*

In this type of sound change, *u* may replace *hi* (pronounced *i*), *bi*, or *mi*. *U-onbin* may occur in the following contexts.

1. The *ren'yōkei* form *hi* of a *ha*-type verb (e.g. omou) may become *u* before *te*. A resultant *ou* or *au* is pronounced *ō*.

Examples:
> *Omo(h)ite* may become *omoute* (pronounced *omōte*)
> *Shitaga(h)ite* may become *shitagaute* (pronounced *shitagōte*)

2. In texts of the Heian and later periods, the same change sometimes occurs before the suffix *keri* and the *so* of *na. . . so.*

Examples:
> *Tama(h)ikeri* may become *tamaukeri*
> *Na nomasetamai so* may become *na nomasetamau so*

3. In late Heian and later texts, *u* somtimes replaces the *ren'yōkei* form *bi* or *mi* of a *ba*-type or *ma*-type yodan verb (e.g. tobu, nomu) before *te* or *ta*. The following "t" becomes "d."

Examples:
> *Asobitamau* may become *asoudamau*
> *Tabite* may become *taude*
> *Tsukamite* may become *tsukaude*

Note: In texts of the Heian and later periods, *tsukae* (the *ren'yōkei* of the *shimo nidan* verb tsukau) sometimes becomes *tsukau* (pronounced *tsukō*) when it combines with *matsuru* in the common humble verb tsukaematsuru. *Tsukaumatsuru* is also sometimes encountered in the abbreviated form *tsukamatsuru*.

C. *Hatsu-Onbin* 撥音便 (Also Called *Haneru Onbin*)

N may replace the *ren'yōkei* form *bi* or *mi* of a *ba*-type or *ma*-type *yodan* verb (e.g. yobu, yomu), the *ren'yōkei* form *ni* of a *nahen* verb (e.g. shinu), or, under special conditions (3 below), the *ren'yōkei ri* of a *ra*-type *yodan* verb (e.g. owaru). Such a sound change is called *hatsu-onbin* (skipping sound change).

Hatsu-onbin began to occur early in the Heian period and became very common from late Heian on. It may appear in one of the following contexts.

1. Before *te*. The "t" becomes "d."

> Examples:
> > *Yobite* may become *yonde*
> > *Kumite* may become *kunde*
> > *Shinite* may become *shinde*

2. Before *tari*. The "t" becomes "d."

> Example:
> > *Susumitari* may become *susundari*

3. When the *ren'yōkei* form *ri* of a *ra*-type *yodan* verb is followed by a syllable beginning with *n*.

> Example:
> > *Owarinu* may become *owannu*
> > *Sarinuru* may become *sannuru*

4. When the *ren'yōkei* form *ni* or *mi* of a *nahen* or *ma*-type *yodan* verb is followed by the *shi* or *shika* form of the suffix *ki*. "Sh" becomes "j."

> Examples:
> > *Inishi* may become *inji*
> > *Konomishika* may become *kononjika*

D. *Soku-Onbin* 促音便 (Also Called *Tsumaru Onbin*)

Soku-onbin (compression sound change) is the term used to designate compression of the *ren'yōkei* form *chi*, *hi*, or *ri* of a *ta*-type, *ha*-type, or *ra*-type *yodan* verb (e.g. utsu, omou, noru), or of the *ren'yōkei* form *ri* of a *rahen* verb (e.g. ari). It may occur before a syllable beginning with "t."

> Examples:
> > *Kachite* may become *katte*
> > *Shitagaite* may become *shitagatte*

> *Shirite* may become *shitte*
> *Arite* may become *atte*

II. Onbin in Adjectives

Japanese adjectives exhibit three of the above four types of sound change: *i-onbin*, *u-onbin*, and *hatsu-onbin*.

A. *I-Onbin*

In this type of sound change, *i* replaces the *rentaikei* form *ki* or *shiki*.

1. *I-onbin* occurs most frequently when the adjective is followed by a substantive.

   Examples:
   > Ito kara*ki* koto nari may become ito kara*i* koto nari
   > Ao*ki* karaginu may become ao*i* karaginu

2. It also appears in other contexts; for example, before the exclamatory *ka na*.

   Example:
   > Kanashi*ki* ka na may become kanashi*i* ka na

B. *U-Onbin*

In this type of sound change, *u* replaces the *ren'yōkei ku* or *shiku*. The change occurs most frequently when the adjective is followed by an inflectable word—i.e. by another adjective, by a verb, or by a suffix. The resultant vowel combinations *au*, *iu*, *eu*, and *ou* are pronounced *o*, *[y]ū*, *yō*, and *ō* respectively.

   Examples:
   > Aka*ku* nareba may become aka*u* (akō) nareba
   > Ayashi*ku* mezurashiki koto may become ayashi*u* (ayashū) mezura-shiki koto
   > Be*ku* sōrau may become be*u* (byō) sōrau
   > Yuki shiro*ku* miyu may become yuki shiro*u* (shirō) miyu

C. *Hatsu-Onbin*

In this type of sound change, *n* replaces the final syllable *ru* of a *rentaikei* form *karu* or *shikaru* before such suffixes as *nari*, *beshi*, *meri*, and *rashi*.

   Examples:
   > Hito*shikaru* nari may become hitoshika*n* nari
   > Kata*karu* beshi may become kataka*n* beshi

TABLE I
MODERN VERB CATEGORIES AND THEIR BASES

Verb Category	Examples from Various Kana Lines (Dic'ty Forms)	Stem	Base Endings				
			Mizenkei 未然形	Ren'yokei 連用形	Shūshikei/ Rentaikei 終止形/連体形	Izenkei (Kateikei) 己然形 (仮定形)	Meireikei 命令形
Yodan 四段	osu (push)	o-	-sa	-shi	-su	-se	-se
	utsu (hit)	u-	-ta	-chi	-tsu	-te	-te
	omou (think)	omo-	-wa	-(h)i	-(f)u	(h)e	-(h)e
	shinu (die)	shi-	-na	-ni	-nu	-ne	-ne
	nomu (drink)	no-	-ma	-mi	-mu	-me	-me
	aru (have)	a-	-ra	-ri	-ru	-re	-re
Kami Ichidan 上一段	kiru (wear)	—	ki	ki	kiru	kire	ki
	ochiru (fall)	o-	-chi	-chi	-chiru	-chire	-chi
	hajiru (feel shame)	ha-	-ji	-ji	-jiru	-jire	-ji
	miru (see)	—	mi	mi	miru	mire	mi
Shimo Ichidan 下一段	ueru (plant)	u-	-e	-e	-eru	-ere	-e
	ukeru (receive)	u-	-ke	-ke	-keru	-kere	-ke
	taberu (eat)	ta-	-be	-be	-beru	-bere	-be
Sahen サ変	suru (do)	—	se, shi, sa	shi	suru	sure	se, shi
Kahen カ変	kuru (come)	—	ko	ki	kuru	kure	ko

Notes

1. Stem plus base ending yields base. To find the stem of a *yodan* verb, subtract the last kana syllable of the dictionary form (*shūshikei*). For the stem of any other MJ verb, subtract the last two syllables, which in some cases will leave nothing, showing that base endings and bases are identical. The kana-line (*gyō* 行) represented in the verb's final syllable (for *yodan* verbs) or penultimate syllable (for others) appears in the initial syllable of the base ending. For examples of verbs ending in syllables of kana-lines not represented here, see *Kōjien* 広辞苑, ed. Shinmura Izuru 新村出 (Iwanami Shoten 岩波書店, 1976), p. 2396.

2. The *yodan* category is called four-step because its bases end in the four vowels *a, i, u,* and *e*. When suffixes beginning with "t" are added to the *ren'yōkei* of this category only, the following sound changes occur regularly in MJ, EXCEPT before *-tai*. Note that these rules apply only to MJ. For changes that *may* occur in literary Japanese, see "Sound Changes (*Onbin*) in Verbs and Adjectives."

   a. *Ki* becomes *i* (e.g. *kikite* becomes *kiite*).

   b. *Gi* becomes *i* and the following "t" changes to "d" (e.g. *oyogite* becomes *oyoide*).

   c. *Bi*, *ni*, or *mi* becomes *n* and the "t" becomes "d" (e.g. *erabite* becomes *erande*; *shinite*, *shinde*; *yomite*, *yonde*).

   d. *Chi*, *(h)i*, and *ri* are replaced by "t" (e.g. *uchite* becomes *utte*; *ka(h)ite*, *katte*; *arite*, *atte*).

3. The *kamiichidan* category is called one-step because it is based on a single vowel (*i*); "upper" because *i* precedes *e* in the kana table. Not all verbs ending in *-iru* belong to this category; some are *yodan* (e.g. hairu, enter; chiru, scatter). When in doubt, consult a dictionary.

4. The *shimoichidan* category is called lower one-step because *e* comes after *i* in the kana table. Some verbs ending in *-eru* belong to the *yodan* category (e.g. kaeru, return).

5. *Sahen* is an abbreviation of *sagyō henka katsuyō* サ行変化活用 (*sa*-line inflectional category). The only verbs in the category are suru and its sonant form -zuru. -Zuru has only two *mizenkei* forms, *ze* and *ji*.

6. *Kahen* is an abbreviation of *kagyō henka katsuyō* カ行変化活用 (*ka*-line inflectional category). The only verb in the category is kuru.

TABLE II
USES OF MODERN VERB BASES

Base	Uses
Mizenkei	Takes suffixes indicating negation, doubt, conjecture, intention; serves as base for passive, potential, polite, and causative forms
Ren'yōkei	Adverbial, continuative, connective
Shūshikei	Sentence-ending form; dictionary form
Rentaikei	Attributive form (precedes substantives)
Izenkei (Kateikei)	Usually appears as a base for *ba* (if, when)
Meireikei	Imperative

Notes

1. The *mizenkei* never stands alone. Common suffixes: *mai* (affixed to *mizenkei* of all except *yodan* verbs), *nai, n(u), u, (ra)reru, (sa)seru*. For the *u* suffix, sound changes produce such forms as yomō, miyō, tabeyō.
2. The *ren'yōkei* may appear with or without suffixes. When alone, it may function as a substantive. At the end of a clause, it indicates that another clause will follow. Common suffixes: *te, ta, tari, tara, tai, masu.*
3. The *shūshikei* and *rentaikei* have different uses but identical forms in modern Japanese. They usually stand alone. Suffixes: *mai* (with *yodan* verbs only), *beshi.*
4. The *izenkei*, which has the alternative name *kateikei* in MJ only, sometimes stands alone after the emphatic particle *koso*. Otherwise it is always followed by a suffix. The most common *izenkei* suffix is *ba.*
5. The *meireikei* stands alone, except that with some verbs, mostly *ichidan*, it is customary to add an emphatic particle (*ro, yo,* or *i*).

TABLE III
LITERARY VERB AND ADJECTIVE CATEGORIES AND THEIR BASES

A. VERBS

| Verb Category | Examples | | Stem | Mizenkei 未然形 | Ren'yōkei 連用形 | Base Endings | | | |
	Bungo Dict'y Form	Corresponding MJ Form				Shūshikei 終止形	Rentaikei 連体形	Izenkei 已然形	Meireikei 命令形
Yodan	yuku (go)	yuku	yu-	-ka	-ki	-ku	-ku	-ke	-ke
Kami Ichidan	miru (see)	miru	mi-	—	—	-ru	-ru	-re	—
Kami Nidan	oku (rise)	okiru	o-	-ki	-ki	-ku	-kuru	-kuré	-ki
	otsu (fall)	ochiru	o-	-chi	-chi	-tsu	-tsuru	-tsure	-chi
	mochiyu (use)	mochiiru	mochi-	-[y]i	-[y]i	-yu	-yuru	-yure	-[y]i
	hazu (feel shame)	hajiru	ha-	-ji	-ji	-zu	-zuru	-zure	-ji
Shimo Ichidan	keru (kick)	keru	ke-	—	—	-ru	-ru	-re	—
Shimo Nidan	uku (receive)	ukeru	u-	-ke	-ke	-ku	-kuru	-kure	-ke
	sutsu (discard)	suteru	su-	-te	-te	-tsu	-tsuru	-tsure	-te
	miyu (be visible)	mieru	mi-	-[y]e	-[y]e	-yu	-yuru	-yure	-[y]e
	izu (leave)	deru	-i	-de	-de	-zu	-zuru	-zure	-de
	fu (pass)	heru	—	he	he	fu	furu	fure	he
	kangau (think)	kangaeru	kanga-	-e	-e	-u	-uru	-ure	-e
Kahen	ku (come)	kuru	—	ko	ki	ku	kuru	kure	ko
Sahen	su (do)	suru	—	se	shi	su	suru	sure	se
Nahen	shinu (die)	shinu	shi	-na	-ni	-nu	-nuru	-nure	-ne
Rahen	ari (have)	aru	a-	-ra	-ri	-ri	-ru	-re	-re

83

Notes

1. Stem plus base ending yields base. For *bungo* verbs, the stem can most conveniently be defined as the form obtained by subtracting the last kana syllable of the *bungo* dictionary form. The kana-line (*gyō* 行) represented in the verb's final syllable appears in the initial syllable of the base ending. A fairly large number of *bungo* verbs belong to more than one category. To determine category, consult *Kōjien* (see Table I above) or a similar dictionary.

2. *Bungo* and MJ forms are identical for *yodan* verbs. Most verbs belonging to this category in MJ also belong to it in *bungo*.

3. *Bungo* and MJ forms are identical for *kamiichidan* verbs; however, this is a very small category in *bungo*. Main verbs: miru (see), niru (resemble, boil), kiru (wear), hiru (dry), iru (sit, shoot).

4. Most MJ *kamiichidan* verbs occur in *bungo* as *kaminidan*. There is no *kaminidan* category in MJ.

5. *Bungo* and MJ forms are identical for *shimoichidan* verbs; however, keru is the only *shimoichidan* verb in the literary language.

6. Most MJ *shimoichidan* verbs occur in *bungo* as *shimonidan*. There is no *shimonidan* in MJ.

7. There are only two *nahen* verbs, shinu (die) and inu (go).

8. In addition to *ari*, the small *rahen* category includes nari (MJ de aru), ori (be), and haberi (polite equivalent of ari).

TABLE III–CONT.

B. INFLECTED ADJECTIVES

Inflectional Category	Dict'y Form Bungo	Dict'y Form MJ	Stem	Mizenkei	Ren'yōkei	Shūshikei	Base Endings Rentaikei	Izenkei	Meireikei
Ku-type	takashi	takai	taka-	-ku, -kara	-ku, -kari	-shi	-ki, -karu	-kere	—, -kare
	nashi	nai	na-	-ku, -kara	-ku, -kari	-shi	-ki, -karu	-kere	—, -kare
Shiku-type	suzu-shi	suzu-shii	suzu-shii-	-ku, -kara	-ku, -kari	—	-ki, -karu	-kere	—, -kare

Notes

1. Stem plus base ending yields base. Inflected *bungo* adjectives fall into two categories, as shown in the table. For the first (ku-type), the stem is obtained by subtracting the last syllable of the *bungo* dictionary form (*shūshikei*). For the second (shiku-type), the stem is identical with the dictionary form. For the *mizenkei* of both types, the most commonly encountered form is *kara*, a contraction of *ku* plus *ara*, the *mizenkei* of *ari*. Similar contractions with *ari* occur with the *ren'yōkei, rentaikei,* and *meireikei.* In texts of the Nara period, *ke* occasionally appears as a *mizenkei* or *izenkei* base ending.

2. An adjective stem sometimes stands alone. Thus:
   Iya *tō* ni: Ever more *distant.*(MYS)
   Ana, *medeta* no Giō gozen no saiwai ya: Ah, what *splendid* fortune Lady Gio enjoys! (*Heike*)

3. The stem of a MJ inflected adjective is obtained by subtracting the final syllable of the MJ dictionary form—e.g. *ao* from *aoi, yakamashi* from *yakamashii.* The MJ base endings are *ku, ku, i, i, kere,* —.

TABLE IV
FORMS OF COMMON INFLECTED LITERARY SUFFIXES

Suffix	Added To	Mizen.	Ren'yo.	Shūshi.	Rentai.	Izen.	Meirei.	Remarks
Beshi	shūshi.[1]	beku, bekara	beku, bekari	beshi	beki, bekaru, bekan, beka	bekere	—	Ku-type adj. Alternative mizen. beke, ren'yō. byō and bemi, rentai. bei. Also special Heian form beranari (incomplete rahen). Beshi normally follows extended rentai. of adj. (e.g. yokarubeshi).
Gotoshi	rentai., ga, no	[gotoku]	gotoku	gotoshi	gotoki	—	—	Gotoki may appear in adverbial position; gotoku may be followed by ni. A form other than rentai. may precede suffix nari.
Kemu	ren'yō.	—	—	kemu	kemu	keme	—	
Keri	ren'yō.	kera	—	keri	keru	kere	—	Incomplete rahen
Ki	ren'yō.[2]	[ke], se	—	ki	shi	shika	—	Observe irreg. forms with ku and su (note 2).
Mahoshi	mizen.	maho-shiku	maho-shiku	maho-shi	maho-shiki	maho-shikere	—	Shiku-type adj.
Maji	shūshi.[1]	majikara	majiku, majikari	maji	majiki	majikere	—	Shiku-type adj.
Mashi	mizen.	mashika, mase	—	mashi	mashi	mashika	—	
Meri	shūshi.[1]	—	meri	meri	meru	mere	—	Incomplete rahen
Mu, n	mizen.	[ma]	—	mu, n	mu, n	me	—	Incomplete yodan
Muzu, nzu, uzu	mizen.	—	—	muzu	muzuru	muzure	—	Incomplete sahen
Nari	rentai., substantives	nara	nari, ni	nari	naru	nare	—	Shitei nari
Nari	shūshi.[1]	—	—	nari	naru	nare	—	Denbun/suitei nari

Suffix	Added To	Mizen.	Ren'yō.	Shūshi.	Rentai.	Izen.	Meirei.	Remarks
Nu	ren'yō.	na	ni	nu	nuru	nure	ne	Nahen
Ramu, ran	shūshi.¹	—	—	ramu	ramu	rame	—	Incomplete yodan
Raru	mizen.³	rare	rare	raru	raruru	rarure	rare	Shimo nidan
Rashi	shūshi.,¹ substantive, adj. stem	—	—	rashi	rashi, rashiki	rashi, rashikere	—	
Ri	"meirei."	ra	ri	ri	ru	re	re	Rahen
Ru	mizen.³	re	re	ru	ruru	rure	re	Shimo nidan
Sasu	mizen.³	sase	sase	sasu	sasuru	sasure	sase	Shimo nidan
Shimu	mizen.	shime	shime	shimu	shimuru	shimure	shime	Shimo nidan
Su	mizen.³	se	se	su	suru	sure	se	Shimo nidan
Tari	ren'yō.	tara	tari	tari	taru	tare	tare	Rahen. Completion (kanryō) tari, a contraction of -te ari
Tari	substantives	tara	tari	tari	taru	tare	tare	Rahen. Designation (shite) tari, a contraction of to ari. MJ: de aru
Tashi	ren'yō.	taku	taku	tashi	taki	takere	—	Ku-type adj. Same uses as MJ -tai
Tsu	ren'yō.	te	te	tsu	tsuru	tsure	te	Shimo nidan
Zari	mizen.	zara	zari	[zari]	zaru	zare	zare	Rahen
Zu	mizen.	zu	zu	zu	nu	ne	—	Irreg. Rentaikei begins to appear as n in late Muromachi period

1. Added to the *rentaikei* of *rahen* verbs. May be added to the *mizenkei* of *kamiichidan* and *kaminidan* verbs.
2. For the *kahen* verb ku, the known forms are: *koshi* (rentai.), *koshika* (izen.), *kishi* (rentai.), and *kishika* (izen.). For the *sahen* verb su, the known forms are: *shiki* (shūshi.), *seshi* (rentai.), and *seshika* (izen.).
3. *Raru* and *sasu* are added to *ichidan, nidan, kahen,* and *sahen* verbs. *Ru* and *su* are added to *yodan, nahen,* and *rahen* verbs.

TRADITIONAL KANA USAGE AND MODERN PRONUNCIATION

In 1946 the Japanese government modified existing kana usage to make it conform fairly precisely to modern pronunciation. Prior to that time, texts of all periods had preserved many archaic orthographic usages, relics of early Heian phonetic distinctions which had begun to lose their validity by the thirteenth century, if not before. Since post-1946 editions of old texts ordinarily retain the original orthography, the student should be aware of the correspondences listed below.

Traditional Orthography (Rōmaji Equivalents)	Standard Modern Pronunciation	Examples
a (or syllable ending in *a*) plus *u* or *fu*	*ō*	sau = sō; rafu = rō
i (or syllable ending in *i*) plus *u* or *fu*	*yū*	iu = yū; nifu = nyū; shiu = shū; kiu = kyū
u (or syllable ending in *u*) plus *fu*	*u*	kufu = kū; yufu = yū
e (or syllable ending in *e*) plus *u* or *fu*	*yō*	efu = yō; kefu = kyō; sefu = shō; tefu = chō; neu = nyō; hefu = hyō
o (or syllable ending in *o*) plus *fu* or *wo*	*ō*	ofu = ō; kofu = kō; Shimowosa = Shimōsa
kwa and *gwa*	*ka, ga*	kwan = kan; kwashi = kashi
ha (medially or finally)	*wa*	omohazu = omowazu; kaha = kawa
hi, he, and *ho* (medially or finally)	*i, e, o*	omohite = omoite; kaheru = kaeru; ohoshi = ōshi
wi, we, and *wo* (in all positions)	*i, e, o*	wiru = iru; wetori = etori; woru = oru

Abbreviations

Aux.	Auxiliary
Genji	*Genji monogatari*
Heike	*Heike monogatari*
Hon.	Honorific
Intr.	Intransitive
Ise	*Ise monogatari*
KKS	*Kokinshū*
Mak.	*Makura no sōshi*
MJ	Modern Japanese
MYS	*Man'yōshū*
Take.	*Taketori monogatari*
Tosa	*Tosa nikki*
Tr.	Transitive
TZG	*Tsurezuregusa*
V	Verb

CORNELL UNIVERSITY EAST ASIA SERIES

For information on ordering the preceding publications
and tapes, please write to:

EAST ASIA SERIES
East Asia Program
Cornell University
140 Uris Hall
Ithaca, NY 14853-7601